1987

SCIENCE AND LITERATURE IN THE
NINETEENTH CENTURY

CONTEXT AND COMMENTARY

Series Editor: ARTHUR POLLARD

SCIENCE AND LITERATURE IN THE NINETEENTH CENTURY

J.A.V Chapple

MACMILLAN

First published 1986

Published by
MACMILLAN EDUCATION LTD
Houndmills, Basingstoke, Hampshire RG21 2XS
and London
Companies and representatives
throughout the world

Typeset by
Wessex Typesetters
(Division of The Eastern Press Ltd)
Frome, Somerset

Printed in Hong Kong

British Library Cataloguing in Publication Data
Chapple, J.A.V.
   Science and Literature in the Nineteenth Century
   —(Context and commentary)
   1. English literature—19th century—History
   and criticism   2. Science in literature
   I. Title   II. Series
   820.9'356   PR468.S34
ISBN 0–333–37586–6
ISBN 0–333–37587–4 Pbk

Contents

Acknowledgements

I must thank the staff of the Brynmor Jones University Library at Hull and of the Cambridge University Library for all the help they have so professionally given me. I am also grateful to my colleagues and the University of Hull for a period of study leave during the 1984–85 session and, for a variety of help, to the following individuals: Gillian Beer, John Beer, Alan Bower, G.N. Cantor, John Christie, George Cole, Tess Cosslett, Gill Cowper, Ruth Green, Robin Headlam Wells, A.M. Hughes, Owen Knowles, Angela Leighton, Greg Myers, Marion Shaw, Sally Shuttleworth and Christopher Strachan. Some of this assistance was so informally sought that I make the usual statement of personal responsibility for all faults and errors with unusual emphasis. Yet again, I am pleased to acknowledge the constant encouragement and good advice of Arthur Pollard. James Chapple helped to compile the index. My deepest thanks must go to my wife, who in a world that seems to be ruled by John Herschel's 'law of higgledy-piggledy', has done her best to make things what she would like them to be, Just So.

List of Plates

1. Humphry Davy (1778–1829) in 1804.
   Photograph © Royal Institution.

2. T.H. Huxley (1825–1895) lecturing in the early 1860s.
   Photograph © Wellcome Institute Library, London.

3. Alfred Tennyson (1809–92) in c.1840 by S. Laurence.
   Photograph © National Portrait Gallery.

4. Charles Robert Darwin (1809–82), after the portrait by Maguire c.1850.
   Photograph © BBC Hulton Picture Library.

5. Faraday lecturing at the Royal Institution before the Prince Consort and the Prince of Wales.
   Photograph © Royal Institution.

6. How the elephant got its trunk as featured in the *Just So Stories*, 1902, by Rudyard Kipling © Bodleian Library, Oxford.

7. The frontispiece to T.H. Huxley's *Evidence as to Man's place in Nature* (1863) which shows four skeletons progressing from a gibbon to a man.

Editor's Preface

J.H. Plumb has said that 'the aim of (the historian) is to understand men both as individuals and in their social relationships in time. "Social" embraces all of man's activities – economic, religious, political, artistic, legal, military, scientific – everything, indeed, that affects the life of mankind.' Literature is itself similarly comprehensive. From Terence onwards writers have embraced his dictum that all things human are their concern.

It is the aim of this series to trace the interweavings of history and literature, to show by judicious quotation and commentary how those actually working within the various fields of human activity influenced and were influenced by those who were writing the novels, poems and plays within the several periods. An attempt has been made to show the special contribution that such writers make to the understanding of their times by virtue of their peculiar imaginative 'feel' for their subjects and the intensely personal angle from which they observe the historical phenomena that provide their inspiration and come within their creative vision. In its turn the historical evidence, besides and beyond its intrinsic importance, serves to 'place' the imaginative testimony of the writers.

The authors of the several volumes in this series have sought to intermingle history and literature in the conviction that the study of each is enhanced thereby. They have been free to adopt their own approach within the broad general pattern of the series. The topics themselves have sometimes also a particular slant and emphasis. Commentary, for instance, has had to be more detailed in some cases than in others. All the contributors to the series are at one, however, in the belief (at a time when some critics would not only divorce texts from their periods but even from their authors) that literature is the creation of actual men and women, actually living in an identifiable set of historical circumstances, themselves both the creatures and the creators of their times.

ARTHUR POLLARD

Introduction

Science and Sciences in the Nineteenth Century

The word *science* once meant knowledge acquired by study. Not until the nineteenth century did its meaning tend to be restricted to the systematic study of the material and natural universe. Early scientists were usually called 'natural philosophers' but in 1840 William Whewell wrote in his *Philosophy of the Inductive Sciences* 'We need very much a name to describe a cultivator of science in general. I should incline to call him a Scientist.' Incredible as it may now seem, that is the very first use of the word *scientist* cited in the Oxford English Dictionary. Whewell had actually used it some years earlier, when reviewing Mary Somerville's *On the Connexion of the Physical Sciences*. He describes what must have been a lively discussion at the third annual meeting of the newly founded British Association for the Advancement of Science, held at Cambridge in 1833:

> *Philosophers* was felt to be too wide and too lofty a term, and was very properly forbidden them by Mr. Coleridge, both in his capacity of philologer and metaphysician; *savans* was rather assuming, besides being French instead of English; some ingenious gentleman proposed that, by analogy with *artist*, they might form *scientist*, and added that there could be no scruple in making free with this termination when we have such words as *sciolist*, *economist*, and *atheist* – but this was not generally palatable; .... .
>
> *Quarterly Review*, Vol. 51, 1834, p.59.

Coleridge had at one time used the words *philosopher* and *bard* for 'scientist' and 'poet', but long before, in his poem 'Religious Musings' of 1794. Whewell's learned fun – he may

1

well have been the 'ingenious gentleman' who ironically raised scientists to the dignity of artists but then forced them to associate with mere pretenders to knowledge, economists and atheists – does not disguise from us the felt need for a word that would express a growing sense of professional independence amongst 'men of science' and, if we look back in Whewell's review and reflect upon the title of Mrs Somerville's book, help compensate for what Whewell called the 'disintegration' of physical science as it fell into apparently endless, insulated sub-divisions. Attacked much later as an American barbarism by T.H. Huxley, who thought it 'about as pleasing a word as "Electrocution" ', and considered to be a colloquialism even into this century, *scientist* survived. (See Sydney Ross, '*Scientist*: the Story of a Word', *Annals of Science*, Vol. 18, 1962, pp.65-85.)

It is worth remembering that at the beginning of the nineteenth century some sciences did not exist in any formal sense and that others were changing their nature. Astronomy and botany remain much what they were in the seventeenth century but the old science of chemistry, though well through its mystical, alchemical phase, was only just being distinguished from physics. Physics itself had once meant the study of the whole natural universe, organic as well as inorganic, but during the course of the eighteenth century it became more focused on the latter. As Whewell wrote in his review of Mrs Somerville, 'the chemist is perhaps a chemist of electro-chemistry; if so, he leaves common chemical analysis to others; between the mathematician and the chemist is to be interpolated a '*physicien*' (we have no English name for *him*), who studies heat, moisture, and the like' (p.59). Another of Whewell's inventions, 'physicist', is a sign that a major branch of science had achieved its distinctive scope and pattern of understanding – at least until recent years, since it is again extending its range into the organic world. Geology, too, emerged towards the end of the eighteenth century from fossil-collecting, landscape description, Biblical theories of the earth's origin and the like to become the science as we know it today, now the study of planetary crusts. 'Biology' is a word borrowed by us from the German *Biologie* in 1819. Its originators wished to distinguish it as a science of living organisms from natural history, which was primarily concerned with classification and description. The sense of excitement felt by those who developed new sciences is as strong as the 'quickening life' we find expressed in contemporary Romantic poetry, even in one of its great elegies, when

> . . . the green lizard and the golden snake,
> Like unimprisoned flames, out of their trance awake.

P.B. Shelley, Adonais (1821), stanza 18.

Appropriately, the later eighteenth century saw a fundamental change in thought about nature, a major instance of which was a definite move away from the view that the individual exists in miniature in the germ to C.F. Wolff's theory that the individual embryo develops, in a self-determined way. In biology, 'preformation' and enlargement of a pre-existing germ gave place to 'epigenesis' and progressive elaboration of a fertilised egg-cell. This was a significant part of the new climate of ideas when Wordsworth was composing his autobiographical 'growth of a poet's mind', *The Prelude*, a poem which itself went through many changes between 1798 and 1850.

The nineteenth century is remarkable for its proliferation of new sciences and sub-sciences, which range from the study of earthquakes (*seismology*, named in 1858) to the study of rudimentary life forms (*embryology*, named in 1859). The acquisition of a special name for a science is usually a sign that it had achieved a distinct professional importance. A tidal wave of fresh observational and experimental knowledge demanded the constant creation of new research and teaching institutes, colleges and university departments, together with the founding of specialised societies and journals. This does not mean, in practice, that the sciences became as hermetically sealed from each other as Whewell affected to fear. Organic chemistry became separated from the main body of chemistry in the early decades of the century, but some was linked with physiology about mid-century and transformed into biochemistry from about 1880. 'Bridge sciences' inevitably sprang up, for there are numerous practical and conceptual links between branches of study only artificially distinguished from each other. Biochemistry cannot be pursued without regard to technological progress in brewing or what M. Teich has called 'the great generalizations' of cell-theory and biological evolution. Nor can science be insulated from the general culture of the age, especially those leading ideas that scientists in several disciplines propose as fundamental truths of life and the universe. For most of the century, belief in some kind of ultimate reality, or uniformity, or regularity, was common to all; few were prepared to speculate that everything was utterly random. But what kinds of order did scientists propose to their contemporaries? The literature of the time shows minutely detailed responses to particular scientific discoveries, as we shall see, but more often it is great conceptual movements that shift the ways in which we apprehend the very nature of reality which are of prime importance; hence the fascination with origins, growth and transformation; the changing awareness of our relation to animals and plants; the new stress placed upon the struggle for existence, progress and extinction; the growing determination to alter circumstances, especially human ones, by discovering how to predict and then change them; and throughout the century the constant desire to find a basic unity of forces and dynamic laws that reconcile or transcend opposites. These movements of thought are less obvious than discrete, precise allusions but they cannot be ignored by any student of the relations between science and literature.

Science in Culture

How did 'creative writers' get to know of scientific discoveries, new hypotheses and procedures? The very fact that Coleridge was an active participant in the third meeting of the British Association, which may have been attended by the young Tennyson, indicates an important organisational means from 1831 onwards, particularly as each annual meeting was held in a different city. A major source must have been the writings of scientists themselves. In the early part of the century chemistry, physics and geology were making exciting advances but in ways that could be appreciated. If readers did not wish to study the actual books published by men like John Dalton, Humphry Davy and Charles Lyell, they could easily refer to the lengthy surveys made for the public at large in the great reviewing journals – *Blackwood's Edinburgh Magazine*, the *Quarterly Review* and the *Edinburgh Review*. They could turn from J.W. Croker's merciless assault on *Poems by Alfred Tennyson* in the April 1833 number of the *Quarterly Review* to Whewell's urbane assessment of Mary Somerville's *Connexion* ('her profound mathematical work on the "Mechanism of the Heavens" has already been treated of in this Journal'), without any feeling that, tone apart, they were moving to a different kind of discourse. It is noticeable that these long reviews are full of substantial quotations. There is often no need to assume that the original scientific works have been consulted by literary authors, even when their wording is identical. We should also bear in mind that many periodicals *are* the original source for both literary and scientific texts – a fact ignored by collectors of first book editions and often unknown to those who only have available modern reprints. Many quotations below have been taken from the journals in which they first appeared, in an attempt to recover the historical moments of a more unified culture which, under increasing strain, lasted through much of the nineteenth century. Sometimes, however, there is good reason to refer to later editions; the policy cannot be rigid.

In the early part of the century a literate reader could understand the chemical articles in the *Annals of Philosophy* or in its successor, the more general *Philosophical Magazine*. But chemistry is a clear example of a science which became more quantitative and, in addition, developed a symbolic language, meaningless to the uninstructed. Similarly, the increasing difficulty and complication of many sciences ensured that the work of popularisers flourished, at all levels. The highest might be that of Mary Somerville, who would be almost as famous as Florence Nightingale or George Eliot if general historians had ever paid much attention to science. She was, in fact, not so much a populariser as an expositor, capable of the very highest quality work, though a sad little manuscript draft of her

Personal Recollections (1873) avows, 'I was conscious that I had never made a discovery myself, that I had no originality. I have perseverance and intelligence but no genius, that spark from heaven is not granted to the sex, ...' (E.C. Patterson, 'Mary Somerville', *British Journal for the History of Science*, Vol. 4, 1968–69, p.318.) But like Falstaff, she was the cause of wit in others: her writing inspired J.C. Adams to make a major astronomical discovery, the path of an unknown planet, Neptune, and her *Mechanism of the Heavens* (1831) was used in the advanced mathematical classes at Cambridge. More typical would be some of Maria Edgeworth's books for children or Jane Marcet's *Conversations on Chemistry, Intended more especially for the Female Sex*, 2 vols, (1806). It reached a sixteenth edition by 1853 and is said to have sold 160 000 copies in the United States by that date. The blacksmith's son Michael Faraday, who became the greatest experimental scientist of his age, was introduced to electrochemistry by these volumes in 1810, but in this context we should appreciate the wide availability of scientific knowledge and the inevitable similarity of popularisations to forms of creative literature. The vogue for teaching through dialogues and tales is seen in Mrs Marcet's *Conversations – on Natural Philosophy*, on *Vegetable Physiology* and on *Political Economy* (1816), the last of which inspired Harriet Martineau's *Illustrations of Political Economy* (1832–34). 'A Manchester Strike', in Volume 3, is not much of a story in itself but it is a step on the way to a new sub-genre of fiction, the social-problem novel of the 1840s as written by authors like Disraeli, Kingsley and Elizabeth Gaskell.

Science was very much integrated with the culture of its age during the early decades of the nineteenth century. Jane Marcet wrote for an audience created by Coleridge's friend Humphry Davy, brilliant lecturer at the Royal Institution in London, established in 1799 to spread practical knowledge (L.P. Williams, *Michael Faraday* (1965), p.19). The Institution soon turned into a centre at the leading edge of chemical research, Faraday's university in effect, which also provided lectures for a fashionable audience, but its original intention was fulfilled by the Natural History Societies, Literary and Philosophical Societies and various kinds of institute that sprang up in every large town. Scientific knowledge was not the preserve of a special class. Neither the lack of a formal education nor that of an early scientific training could prevent intelligent men and women, like Faraday and Somerville, from contributing powerfully to its advancement. Elizabeth Gaskell's portrayal of Manchester workmen studying mayflies in the annual Whitsun-week holiday (*Mary Barton* (1848), Chapter 5), together with the comical picture she conjures up of one man begging his daughter not to drop the flat-iron on a scorpion found torpid in the Liverpool docks but warmed into life by the heat of the kitchen fire, is every bit as representative as Charles Darwin's voyage of 1831–36 to the Galapagos Archipelago or Alfred Wallace's travels of 1854–62 about the Malayan Archipelago. They were engaged in a common enterprise and informed by the same ethos. Beside the *Transactions* and *Proceedings* of learned societies, there bloomed numerous commercial periodicals like the *Annals of Natural History*, which Darwin did not disdain to read and cite. Admittedly Darwin and Wallace propounded one of the most important scientific theories of modern times, evolution by means of natural selection, and the fame Darwin achieved made Elizabeth Gaskell consider him a fit model for the hero of her finest novel, *Wives and Daughters* (1864–66). In the high noon of Victorian optimism scientists are as suitable as captains of industry to play leading roles in the most popular literary form of the age, though Mary Shelley's *Frankenstein* of 1818 can serve as a reminder of an underlying fear of science that was to surface again in Wells's *Doctor Moreau* in the last decade of the century.

The accessibility of science, however, was waning. Darwin continued a tradition of writing for the educated reader in his *Origin of Species* (1859) but some of the controversy it sparked off was very obscure. The mathematical language of Lord Kelvin's physics, his calculations to prove that the earth could not be as old as required for the slow processes of evolution, was, and is, incomprehensible to many. Ironically this includes Darwin, whose letters describe the founder of modern thermodynamics, Kelvin, coming like an 'odious spectre' (12 July 1871) and whose autobiography admits to the common superstition that mathematicians possess an extra sense. Even if both men could have been miraculously informed of later discoveries of radioactivity in the earth and nuclear reactions in the sun, one level of communication would still remain closed. There is a further irony in the fact that Darwin's area of least competence, genetics (*OED*, 1897), was developed by his cousin Francis Galton in a statistical manner, leading to biometry (*OED*, 1901). Galton began by using the marks obtained in a Cambridge University mathematics examination (senior wrangler 7634, lowest honours man 237) as evidence of the extraordinary range of ability to be found in one of the highest groups of the population (*Hereditary Genius* (1869), p.19). Its significance must be qualified, of course, by the occurrence of geniuses like Macaulay, who found in mathematics 'starvation, confinement, torture, annihilation of the mind' (letter of 24 February 1819), and Darwin, who failed to obtain honours at Cambridge and took a pass degree. Though the mathematician George Boole, inventor of Boolean algebra and admirer of Dante's *Paradiso*, wrote a 'Sonnet to the Number Three' (*Mind*, Vol. 57, 1948, p.157) and his system is used for non-mathematical operations, one might roughly claim that science in mathematical or symbolic form is alien to literature. The mathematical lecturer at Christ Church, Oxford, C.L. Dodgson, is not known to the reading public for his works on geometry, trigonometry and determinants but for his two *Alice* books of 1865 and 1872. His professional powers there reveal themselves indirectly, in the logical puzzles of Wonderland – a grin without a cat, Nobody passed on the road, lessons lessening from day to day, or the White Queen living backwards and believing as many as six impossible things before breakfast. It is more like twentieth-century physics.

Efforts were made. General periodicals, often appearing monthly or weekly, provided a forum for scientific articles – *Macmillan's Magazine*, the *Leader*, *Household Words*, the *Fortnightly Review*, the *Contemporary Review* and the *Nineteenth Century* amongst others. Some have special interest for us. George Eliot helped with the editing of the *Westminster Review* when it was refounded in 1852, for instance. Early issues included 'The Future of Geology' and 'Plants and Botanists' by the naturalist Edward Forbes, 'The

Lady Novelists' and 'Goethe as a Man of Science' by her companion-to-be, G.H. Lewes, who could write expertly enough on almost any subject. Together they became a formidably learned pair, as we can see from Sally Shuttleworth's close study of George Eliot's 'active dialogue' with the advanced thought of the age. In a more relaxed mode certain journals went out to attract readers, very successfully, by serialised fiction. Thackeray's first concern as editor of a new monthly, the *Cornhill Magazine*, was to obtain a variety of attractive contributions. The initial number in January 1860 contained the beginning of Trollope's *Framley Parsonage* and the illustrated opening chapter of Lewes's *Studies in Animal Life*: 'Come with me and lovingly study Nature, as she breathes, palpitates, and works under myriad forms of life – forms unseen, unsuspected, or unheeded by the mass of ordinary men . . . .' (See *Cornhill Magazine*, Vol. 1 (1860), pp.1; 61.) Fiction first, but popular science not too far behind! T.H. Huxley's famous lecture upon a piece of chalk, first delivered to working men in Norwich during a meeting of the British Association, was printed in the September 1868 issue of *Macmillan's Magazine*; the issues of the *Nineteenth Century* for 1889 contained the articles in which he justified his position as an agnostic, a word he himself had coined for one who, whilst not an atheist, could not believe in an unknown and unknowable First Cause. But neither of these articles represent his strictly professional writings – 'On the Morphology of the Cephalous Mollusca . . . .' and the like. R.M. Young tells us that in the latter part of the century the British Association was 'ceasing to serve the function of the expositor of the best science to a glittering audience', the scientific periodical *Nature*, founded in 1869, was attracting substantial articles away from the general press and, increasingly, specialist journals were founded. The establishment of *Mind* in 1876 was followed two years later by *Brain*, a journal for the study of neurology and neurophysiology ('Natural Theology, Victorian Periodicals, and the Fragmentation of a Common Context', in *Darwin to Einstein*, eds C. Chant and J. Fauvel (1980), pp.91-96). A reminiscence of Thackeray's schooldays, printed in the *Cornhill Magazine* for 1865, points the difference: 'We took in the Magazines – *Blackwood*, the *New Monthly*, the *London*, and the *Literary Gazette* – then in nearly their first glory, and full of excellent articles. . . . This was the real commencement of Thackeray's connection with the Magazines, which he used to read with the greatest eagerness, little interfered with by any school responsibilities' (Vol. 11, pp.126-27).

Sciences, however, vary in difficulty. The *Quarterly Review* and the *Edinburgh Review* were in 1825–28 'too high and dry' for the young Thackeray. No doubt sciences like psychology and anthropology were comprehensible, at least until Freud's English translators began inventing terms like *cathexis* and *parapraxis* for his ordinary German words. But perhaps only writers like H.G. Wells, who had taken a London science degree, were comfortable with a range of primary scientific texts in the last decades of the century. Most responded in a broad way to the larger issues and relied more than ever upon intermediaries.

All day with the ship-owners, and in the evening dinner, phonograph, X rays, talk about *the* secret of the Universe, and the nonexistence of, so called, matter. The secret of the universe is in the existence of horizontal waves whose varied vibrations are at the bottom of all states of consciousness. If the waves were vertical the universe would be different. This is a truism. But, don't you see, there is nothing in the world to prevent the simultaneous existence of vertical waves, or waves at any angles; in fact there are mathematical reasons for believing that such waves do exist. Therefore it follows that two universes may exist in the same place and in the same time – . . . .

These things I said to the Dr. [John McIntyre, pioneer radiologist] while Neil Munro stood in front of a Röntgen machine and on the screen behind we contemplated his backbone and his ribs. . . . It was so – said the Doctor – and there is no space, time, matter, mind as vulgarly understood, there is only the eternal something that waves and an eternal force that causes the waves – it's not much – and by the virtue of these two eternities exists that Corot and that Whistler in the diningroom upstairs (we were in a kind of cellar) and Munro's here writings and your Nigger and Graham's politics and Paderewski's playing (in the phonograph) and what more do you want?

29 September 1898; *Letters from Conrad*,
ed. E. Garnett (1928), pp.137-38.

Redmond O'Hanlon rightly associates this letter with another in which Conrad expresses his more philosophically comprehensive belief that 'all is illusion – the words written, the mind at which they are aimed, the truth they are intended to express, the hands that will hold the paper, the eyes that will glance at the lines' (*Joseph Conrad and Charles Darwin: The Influence of Scientific Thought on Conrad's Fiction* (1984), pp.20-22). It also seems likely that Conrad is retailing facts and hypotheses concerning the x-rays just discovered by Röntgen with all the innocent enthusiasm of a man who has found his own views confirmed by a shaman or witch doctor. At the beginning of the century Coleridge had walked with physical scientists as an equal in understanding, if not in authority. To be fair to Conrad, he was writing at a time of exceptional theoretical upheaval in the physical sciences. James Clerk Maxwell's electromagnetic theories, for instance, experimentally based and internally consistent, could not be reconciled with the absolute nature of time and space assumed by Newtonian physics. The radiation he had predicted was in fact detected after his death in 1879, by Hertz, but as G.H.A. Cole explains, Maxwell's wave theory seemed to require an ether, 'an all-pervading fluid-like material', hypothetically more rigid than steel, for its propagation! None could be found. Einstein stated his theory of restricted relativity in 1905 to resolve the conflicts. Other fundamental difficulties led to Max Planck's revolutionary quantum theory of 1900, but these are major achievements of this century. Whewell's belief in 1833 that mechanics, hydrostatics and physical astronomy had 'at least approached their complete and finished form' (*Astronomy and General Physics Considered with Reference to Natural Theology*, p.308) was plausible enough in its day, but in retrospect seems over-complacent. Relativity became the new key to knowledge at the end of the century, and even the possibility of a 'complete and finished' description of the physical world is now problematic, as Cole's lucid exposition of physics from Galileo, Kepler and Newton to Planck and Einstein makes clear ('Physics', in *The Twentieth-Century Mind*, eds C.B. Cox and A.E. Dyson, Oxford (1972), Vol. 1, pp.265-69; 289-93).

Science in Literature

Individual 'creative writers' vary immensely in their knowledge and understanding of science. A.N. Whitehead went so far as to say in 1925 that if 'Shelley had been born a hundred years later, the twentieth century would have seen a Newton amongst chemists' (*Science and the Modern World* (1929), p.105). Carl Grabo wrote a book on Shelley's use of science as long ago as 1930, *A Newton Among Poets*, but recent years have seen a small explosion of such studies, which give an unfamiliar look to literary history. Amongst Romantic poets, Shelley and Coleridge figure more prominently than Wordsworth and Keats. Of the novelists who became so popular in the middle decades of the century, probably George Eliot holds pride of place, though we shall see that Dickens, Disraeli, Charles Kingsley and, later, Hardy, are important. The Brontës have received relatively little attention. A recent article by B.M. Goff, 'Between Natural Theology and Natural Selection: Breeding the Human Animal in *Wuthering Heights*', seems to show that the basic material is recalcitrant. Emily Brontë was 'probably not familiar with the literature of animal husbandry' but one might assume that family lore and local newspapers would have informed her about two particular breeds of sheep, 'even taking into account that the attributes of the two varieties of sheep reverse those of the characters: the ruggedness, fierce eyes, coarse wool, and black faces of Linton sheep being more like Heathcliff, and the fine fleece of the Penistone closer to the features of the Linton characters' (*Victorian Studies*, Vol. 27, 1983–84, pp.496-97). There is a good deal more in the article, of course, but much of it is unavoidably speculative. Goff can say that John Kidd's *On the Adaptation of External Nature to the Physical Condition of Man* was 'available' to Emily Brontë. In *A Strange Story* (Chapter 55) Edward Bulwer-Lytton definitely refers to Kidd's Bridgewater Treatise, one of a series (1833–37) designed to show God's power and wisdom manifest in the creation. Any study of Bulwer's romance can start from the learned footnotes he provided ('Müller, Physiology of the Senses, Baley's translation, pp.1068-1395 . . . .' and the like), despite the incongruous fact that it was serialised in a family periodical, Dickens' *All the Year Round* (10 August 1861–8 March 1862). Both Emily Brontë and Bulwer wrote in a period of transition, between prevailing ideas of a benevolent design in nature and naturalistic explanations based on material causes, but the scientific aspects of this change can only be inferred from *Wuthering Heights*, without much certainty. Bulwer's footnotes are only the most obvious sign of his direct engagement in the problems involved, which he embodies in character, plot and dialogue. This strange and versatile man, who had all the characteristics of a genius without actually being one, was undoubtedly trying to assess fringe sciences and occult phenomena – mesmerism, 'electric biology', phrenology, clairvoyance and apparitions – through the medium of fiction, like some nineteenth-century hybrid of D.H. Lawrence and Arthur Koestler.

There is a temptation to think that the truest relationships between science and literature are to be found in works as committed as some of Bulwer's. It is interesting to view the connection from the other side: to see that the necessary conditions of scientific romances such as Bulwer's *The Coming Race* (1871), those of his contemporary Jules Verne or of H.G. Wells in the 1890s, are present in rudimentary form in another of the Bridgewater Treatises, Whewell's *Astronomy and General Physics* (1833). In an important article, 'Early Victorian Science Writers and Tennyson's "In Memoriam": a Study in Cultural Exchange', Susan Gliserman has analysed the rhetorical strategies of several mediators of science, including Whewell, who, himself a scientist, was also perhaps the most important historian and philosopher of science in the country. He wrote for more than one readership. In his *History of the Inductive Sciences* (1837) he is careful to describe the solar and sidereal universe in terms of mechanistic relationships 'in order to reproduce it as it evolved as a conception in the minds of experimental scientists', but in his Bridgewater Treatise the relationships became 'emotionally significant' as he 'read' the universe in religious terms. To prove God's care he imagined alternative environments which might have afflicted life on earth: the constant state of temperature and sunlight on Saturn, the extreme irregularities of a comet, or the disastrous consequences that would ensue if the earth's surface had been polished iron. In this perspective the whole earth can be thought of 'as employed in keeping a snowdrop in the position most suited to the promotion of its vegetable health', Whewell argues, fancifully. Gliserman quotes one passage in the Treatise which 'gives a definite emotional shape', a fictive structure, to possible derangement in the motion of planets round the sun:

> . . . we might have years of unequal length, and seasons of capricious temperature, planets and moons of portentous size and aspect, glaring and disappearing at uncertain intervals; tides like deluges, sweeping over whole continents; and, perhaps, the collision of two of the planets, and the consequent destruction of all organisation on both of them.

Whewell 'rescues his readers' by showing that the variations are, according to mathematicians, periodic; 'there is built into the system a complex, self-regulating stability' (*Victorian Studies*, Vol. 18, 1974–75; pp.283-95).

We, harrowed by quite different prophecies, can appreciate the likeness between Whewell's subsidiary fictions and the larger inventions of, say, 'The Crystal Egg' and 'The Star', two stories in Wells' *Tales of Time and Space* (1900). It is the scale and number of the latter's imaginative projections that make him so noteworthy for us. His mind was teeming with the ideas, data and implications of science. R.M. Philmus and D.Y. Hughes select from over two hundred items he published between 1887 and 1898 in their edition of his *Early Writings in Science and Science Fiction*. Or we can glance through *The Stolen Bacillus and Other Incidents*, a volume of Wells' short stories that appeared in 1895. The title story is about a bacteriologist; 'A Moth – Genus Novo' concerns the rivalry between two entomologists; 'The Flowering of the Strange Orchid' is based upon 'researches as Darwin did' (p.28); other stories relate to ethnology, physics and mineralogy, palaeontology, zoology, optics and to a splendid Yorkshireman, keeper of three dynamos, who 'doubted the existence of the deity, but accepted Carnot's cycle, and . . . had read Shakespeare and found him weak in chemistry' (p.192)! It is, in fact, another story about racial differences and beliefs, not about Sadi Carnot's theoretical analysis of steam engines in 1824, usually regarded as the beginning of thermodynamics. Even Wells had his limitations.

Cultural Exchange and Shared Discourse

It would, however, be too restrictive to consider only such obvious instances of the interactions between science and literature. Tennyson, for example, responded to science from his early teens.

> Yet know I not your natures, or if that
> Which we call palpable and visible
> Is condensation of firm particles.
> O suns and spheres and stars and belts and systems,
> Are ye or are ye not?
> Are ye realities or semblances
> Of that which men call real?
> Are ye true substance? Are ye anything
> Except delusive shows and physical points
> Endowed with some repulsive potency?
> Could the Omnipotent fill all space, if ye
> Or the least atom in ye or the least
> Division of that atom (if least can dwell
> In infinite divisibility) should be inpenetrable?
> I have some doubt if ye exist when none
> Are by to view ye.

> Lord Tennyson, 'The Devil and the Lady' (c.1824),
> in *Poems*, ed. C. Ricks (1969), pp.29-30.

Commentators naturally refer to the eighteenth-century philosopher Berkeley's proposition that being is to be known, 'or else subsist in the mind of some Eternal Spirit'. We may add that Tennyson seems to be aware, perhaps through a famous Latin poem by Lucretius, of the speculations about the nature of matter which we derive from the ancient Greeks. Democritus held that matter is ultimately composed of tiny, indivisible atoms, whereas his geometrical opponent Anaxagoras maintained that inorganic substances can be divided without end and yet remain the same (*De Rerum Natura*, ll.615-26; 843-46). Tennyson's 'physical points/ Endowed with some repulsive potency' may possibly allude to theories like those of Adam Walker, which are discussed in connection with Shelley in Chapter 1, or even to the subtle and attractive concept of R.J. Boscovich, cautiously introduced in Davy's *Elements of Chemical Philosophy* (1812), that matter is composed of dimensionless points surrounded by alternately attractive and repulsive forces, the latter rising to infinity at the points themselves (Williams, *Michael Faraday*, p.78). Though Davy employs the same adjective as Tennyson, 'physical', a universe composed of such atoms of force would be spectral enough for Tennyson's speaker in this early verse drama.

Coached by his brilliant and erratic father, whose extensive library in the Lincolnshire rectory contained many scientific works as well as the usual classics and theology, and admitted to Trinity College, Cambridge, by no less a man than Whewell, then Fellow and Tutor, later Master and one of the moving spirits in the introduction of a Natural Sciences Tripos at the university, Tennyson might easily have become another Bulwer or Wells. But in his maturity Tennyson became more typical, I think, of creative writers generally, losing touch with the textbook or technical work and often encountering science indirectly through forms of writing invested with intellectual and emotional significance. This becomes progressively more likely as branches of science retire into private symbolic languages of their own, or adopt jargon that never becomes as familiar as Whewell's successful coinages of *anode*, *cathode* and *ion* for Faraday's eleven propositions in electrochemistry of 1834.

Even scientists writing on a more general level can express their intellectual choices in a strangely charged manner:

I ascribe no intention to God, for I mistrust the feeble powers of my reason. I observe facts merely, and go no further. I only pretend to the character of the historian of *what is*. ... I cannot make nature an intelligent being who does nothing in vain, who acts by the shortest mode, who does all for the best.

E. Geoffroy Saint Hilaire, *Philosophie Zoologique*, Paris (1830), p.10.

Whewell cited this passage in order to counteract Saint Hilaire's deliberately limited view of purpose and function, to renew, philosophically, the idea of purposeful design in scientific investigations:

It is well known that the anatomizers of plants and animals, in order to investigate their structure, and to obtain an insight into the grounds why and to what end such parts, ... and exactly such an internal form, come before them, assume, as indispensably necessary, this maxim, that in such a creature *nothing is in vain*, and proceed upon it in the same way in which in general natural philosophy we proceed upon the principle that *nothing happens by chance*.

William Whewell, *History of the Inductive Sciences* (1837), 1847 edn, Vol. 3, pp.512-13.

These passages, Gliserman contends, define a fundamental difference between two scientific viewpoints and attitudes to research, which is later assumed in some of the most impassioned lines of Tennyson's elegy *In Memoriam*, where he can be seen testing the concept of Nature's caring created in the Bridgewater Treatises:

O yet we trust ...
That nothing walks with aimless feet;
That not one life shall be destroy'd,
Or cast as rubbish to the void,
When God hath made the pile complete.

Lord Tennyson, *In Memoriam* (1850), Section 54, ll.1-8.

Had Whewell, Roget and other scientists not brought out the significance of Saint Hilaire's position, Gliserman comments, 'Tennyson would not have been able to use the language of trust and caring with those complex emotional and intellectual resonances which place this poem of personal grief and religious conflict among public and relatively precise scientific discourses' (*Victorian Studies*, Vol. 18, pp.440-41).

A constant stress upon cultural exchange between writers of all kinds directs attention to what actually happened throughout the nineteenth century, enables us to appreciate the variety of interactions between science and literature and, most valuably, places original texts of both in the centre of attention. The common uses of language, modes of expression and 'literary' structures of thought, feeling and invention are all vitally relevant: 'Because of the shared discourse not only *ideas* but metaphors, myths and narrative patterns could move rapidly and freely to and fro between scientists and non-scientists: though not without frequent creative misprision', writes Gillian Beer (*Darwin's Plots: Evolutionary Narrative in Darwin, George Eliot and Nineteenth-Century Fiction* (1983), p.7).

*   *   *

It has not been possible to do more than cover, selectively, the main material and life sciences in this introductory book. Social sciences like the 'political economy' of the early part of the century, sociology, technology, medical practice and so on were immensely important, but they have been considered exhaustively by general historians and, in their interactions with science and literature, by scholars as eminent as Basil Willey, Raymond Williams and Robert Young. Social, political and religious questions cannot be ignored, of course, and they are treated in the sections below whenever they seem essential for a proper understanding of particular relationships between science and literature. Similarly, the many statements made during the century on behalf of Science and Literature (or even, by annexation, Culture) have a certain importance, though more in the realm of public relations than anything else. Various examples have been gathered in Chapter 5, so that they can be considered after at least some of the material that is needed to help form a judgement on their plausibility has been introduced and explained. In this last chapter, too, I have given an analytical account with illustrations of what seems to me to have been the most valuable critical approach developed in recent years.

Inevitably, there are many omissions. To discuss authors like Samuel Butler, Winwoode Reade, Henry Maudsley, Cesare Lombroso, William James and many others would have meant excluding some of those actually considered. In an attempt to mitigate the consequences of such rigorous selection and to build up some sense of the continuities between the Romantic and the Victorian ages (some authors having received various excellent but separate treatments in this context), I have deliberately chosen topics and symbols that recur. Prometheus, harps, the ether, the torpedo and 'the dread Gymnotus' should become reasonably familiar as they reappear, not only in different texts but in different chapters below. It is remarkable how important phrases and terms like *energy, progressive development* and *natural selection* float free of their defining contexts like thistledown, to germinate in strange soils and become part of a completely new ecosystem. From this point of view it is the continuously creative interactions that are exciting. Both science and literature constitute and develop our common culture, a fact that was once perfectly clear when Coleridge was lionised at 'the meeting of the Philosophers at Cambridge' in 1833 and when men of science could not yet bring themselves to adopt the distinction of a special name.

1 Astronomy, Physics, Chemistry, Meteorology

Unity in Diversity

From the time of Galileo in the seventeenth century physical scientists had shown themselves able to reduce masses of data to simple and apparently exact laws, mathematically expressed. Newton's law of gravity in particular accounted for so many otherwise unrelated facts in the heavens and upon earth that it seemed to possess almost scriptural authority. For some, such as the French astronomer and mathematician Laplace, whose *Mécanique Céleste* (1825) was translated and explained for English readers in Mary Somerville's *The Mechanism of the Heavens* (1831), this explanatory power of science led to atheism and materialism. In Britain, however, the broad consensus of opinion is neatly embodied in the full title of a standard work, *Natural Theology: or, Evidences of the Existence and Attributes of the Deity, Collected from the Appearances of Nature* (1802) by William Paley. The alliance between science and religion held firm, though antipathy to science is central to Blake's very personal religion. Scientific thought at the beginning of the century was in consequence unusually confident and open. Manufacturers, miners, clergymen, potters, surveyors, lecturers and many other kinds of people enthusiastically practised science without any fear that it might destroy their faith or upset their neighbours. The relationship between scientists and Romantic poets could be exceptionally close; both were concerned with the natural universe and tended to think about it in similar ways. In such a freely speculative age, words like *motion*, *force* and *power* were variously defined but their conceptual importance was taken for granted and their fundamental unity asserted. They were, too, more than philosophical abstractions. In a letter Coleridge wrote after the death of an infant son early in 1799 he expressed

20

his feelings through ideas of 'vital force' and 'motive Powers' –
all unified for him in *'Life, Power, Being'* and contrasted with a
dead, material universe of mere matter-in-motion.

> My Baby has not lived in vain – this life has been to him
> what it is to all of us, education & developement! . . .
> Death in a doting old age falls upon my feelings ever as a
> more hopeless Phaenomenon than Death in Infancy;
> but *nothing* is hopeless. – What if the vital force which I
> sent from my arm into the stone, as I flung it in the air &
> skimm'd it upon the water – what if even that did not
> perish! – It was *life*–! it was a particle of *Being*–! it was
> *Power*! – & *how could* it perish–? *Life, Power, Being!* –
> organization may & very probably *is*, their *effect*; their
> *cause* it *cannot* be! – I have indulged very curious fancies
> concerning that force, that *swarm* of motive Powers
> which I sent out of my body into that Stone; & which,
> one by one, left the untractable or already possessed
> Mass, ... Oh! this strange, strange, strange Scene-
> shifter, Death! that giddies one with insecurity, & so
> unsubstantiates the living Things that one has grasped
> and handled!–/ Some months ago Wordsworth
> transmitted to me a most sublime Epitaph / whether it
> had any reality, I cannot say. – Most probably, in some
> gloomier moment he had fancied the moment in which
> his Sister might die. . . .

> > A Slumber did my spirit seal,
> > I had no human fears:
> > She seem'd a Thing, that could not feel
> > The touch of earthly years.

> > No motion has she now, no force;
> > She neither hears nor sees,
> > Mov'd round in Earth's diurnal course
> > With rocks, & stones, and trees!

> To Thomas Poole, 6 April 1799, *Collected Letters*,
> ed. E.L. Griggs (1956), Vol. 1, pp.479-80.

Not long after he had written this letter Coleridge met at the
Pneumatic Institution near Bristol a young man who was to

become the most famous chemist of the age for his experimental discoveries and for the intellectual power of his theories about the mysterious energies of the natural world. For a time the young man, Humphry Davy, and Coleridge were the closest of friends. Davy's talents were both literary and scientific; we can find parallels to Coleridge's letter in his poetry and in his textbooks.

> ... whatever view is taken, active powers must be supposed to be bestowed upon some species of matter, and the impulse must be ultimately derived from the same source. In the universe, nothing can be said to be without design. An imperfect parallel may be found in human inventions; springs may move springs, and wheels, indexes; but the motion and the regulation must be derived from the artist; sounds may be produced by undulations in the air, undulations of the air by vibrations of musical strings; but the impulse and the melody must arise from the master.
>
> Humphry Davy, *Elements of Chemical Philosophy* (1812), p.180.

This passage on electrochemical phenomena glides effortlessly into the traditional image of nature as the art of God. Mechanical analogies, we note, are *im*perfect analogies for the active powers of nature displayed in chemical reactions. Davy thought that change must be referred to motion, and motion to active powers, but these powers were *not* 'inherent in or necessarily attached to matter' (D.M. Knight, *The Transcendental Part of Chemistry* (1978), p.69). A poem, written by Davy in about 1808, 'After Recovery from a Dangerous Illness', also takes into account natural powers of growth, light, physical motion and gravitation; it gives a more passionate emphasis to the unity of secondary causes in the universe, actively sustained by God's creative power, the final cause of all. As in Coleridge's letter, important concepts are inescapably scientific; they organise both the theology and the metaphysics of the stanzas quoted, which deal in turn with cosmic forces, divine power and human capacities.

All speaks of change: the renovated forms
   Of long-forgotten things arise again;
The light of suns, the breath of angry storms,
   The everlasting motions of the main.

These are but engines of the Eternal will,
   The One Intelligence, whose potent sway
Has ever acted and is acting still,
   While stars, and worlds, and systems all obey;

Without whose power, the whole of mortal things
   Were dull, inert, an unharmonious band,
Silent as are the harp's untuned strings
   Without the touches of the poet's hand.

A sacred spark created by His breath,
   The immortal mind of man His image bears;
A spirit living 'midst the forms of death,
   Oppressed but not subdued by mortal cares.

> Humphry Davy, 'After Recovery from a
> Dangerous Illness' (c.1808) quoted by Anne Trenner
> in *The Mercurial Chemist: a Life of Sir Humphry
> Davy* (1963), p.97.

In seeking correspondences in nature, scientist and poet were engaged in a common pursuit, typical of the relatively undivided intellectual culture of the age. There had long been a simple analogy made, for instance, between light and sound. Coleridge would perhaps have noticed it afresh when he read a popular scientific survey, translated from the French version of a German original published in 1770.

> This propagation of light is performed in a manner similar to that of sound. A bell, whose sound you hear, by no means emits the particles which enter your ears. You have only to touch it when struck, to be assured that all its parts are in a very sensible agitation. This agitation immediately communicates itself to the more remote particles of air, so that all receive from it

successively a similar motion of vibration, which, reaching the ear, excite in it the sensation of sound. The strings of a musical instrument put the matter beyond all doubt; you see them tremble, go and come. . . .

We find the circumstances, which accompany the sensation of hearing, in a manner perfectly analogous, in that of sight.

The medium only and the rapidity of the vibrations differ. In sound, it is the air through which the vibrations of sonorous bodies are transmitted. But with respect to light, it is the ether [a hypothetical substance], or that medium incomparably more subtile and elastic than air, which is universally diffused wherever the air and grosser bodies leave interstices.

As often, then, as this ether is put into a state of vibration, and is transmitted to the eye, it excites in it the sentiment of vision, which is, in that case, nothing but a similar tremulous motion, whereby the small fibres at the bottom of the eye are agitated.

> Leonhard Euler, transl. H. Hunter, *Letters of Euler to a German Princess* (1795), Vol. 2, pp.76-77.

Coleridge wrote a poem about this time on the Aeolian harp, a stringed instrument that would vibrate musically in the slightest breeze. The final version of this poem, published in 1817, contains eight famous lines. They make use of the sound-light analogy of the previous century but now mere vibrations are raised to powers of nature, human beings are seen as active rather than passive in experience and, as we would expect, a spiritual power is the ground of all being. The vital energies of the human mind are connatural (a favourite word with Coleridge) with the active powers of nature, mysteriously one in their ontological diversity.

> O! the one Life within us and abroad,
> Which meets all motion and becomes its soul,
> A light in sound, a sound-like power in light,
> Rhythm in all thought, and joyance every where –
> Methinks, it should have been impossible

Not to love all things in a world so fill'd;
Where the breeze warbles, and the mute still air
Is Music slumbering on her instrument.

> S.T. Coleridge, 'The Eolian Harp', ll.26-33, *Poems*,
> ed. J. Beer (1974), p.52.

The New Chemistry

In the first decade of the nineteenth century chemistry began to take the place of physical astronomy as the most exciting and significant science. Its implications were thought to be revolutionary. Its significant advances reinforced the growing belief that there was a unity of forces in the natural universe. In the eighteenth century the more elusive phenomena of light, heat, electricity and magnetism had been scientifically explained as the action of different 'elastic fluids or gases' of a hypothetical kind, 'known to us only in their states of motion when acting upon our organs of sense, or upon other matter' (H. Davy, *Elements*, p.66). But in the early spring of 1800 Alessandro Volta announced his invention of the first battery ('the voltaic pile'), which was brilliantly exploited in England to break down ordinary substances chemically. Electricity, which Davy would call an 'etherial substance', not susceptible of being confined or weighed, could decompose ponderable substances – as could heat or light in the infra-red and ultra-violet wavebands discovered at this time. Were all etherial substances manifestations of each other, not fluids but active powers of nature in different forms?

> All the knowledge we possess of external objects is founded upon experience, which furnishes a knowledge of facts, and the comparison of these facts establishes relations, from which, induction, the intuitive belief that like causes will produce like effects, leads us to general laws.
>
> Mrs Somerville, *Mechanism of the Heavens* (1831),
> p.v.

Davy used the 'voltaic pile' to make discoveries of completely new elements – sodium, potassium, magnesium, strontium, calcium, boron, barium and silicon. The active powers involved, however, could be used for synthesis as well as analysis: 'Of Electrical Attraction and Repulsion, and their Relations to Chemical Changes' and 'On Chemical Attraction, and the Laws of Combination and Decomposition' are typical section headings in *Elements*. In a letter written soon after some of Davy's first major discoveries, Coleridge indicates not only the interest and potential he saw in Davy's scientific procedures but also their creative significance.

> By the aid and application of his own great discovery, of the identity of electricity and chemical attractions, he has placed all the elements and all their inanimate combinations in the power of man; . . . . He has proved, too, that by a practicable increase of electric energy all *ponderable* compounds (in opposition to *Light* & *Heat*, magnetic fluid, &c.) may be decomposed, & presented simple – & recomposed thro' an infinity of new combinations. . . . This account will probably interest William . . . .

S.T. Coleridge to Dorothy Wordsworth, 24 November 1807, *Collected Letters*, Vol. 3, p.662.

Davy's electrochemistry was multiplying the possibilities of the subject, both in theory and in practice. He employed, too, a dynamic structure of ideas of combination, affinity, attraction, exchange, repulsion and decomposition which Trevor H. Levere suggests was a reflection for Coleridge of the complex nature and action of human creativity. The relevance of scientific thought to Coleridge's celebrated definition of the literary imagination (called 'secondary' below) is not always sufficiently stressed.

> The IMAGINATION then I consider either as primary or secondary. The primary IMAGINATION I hold to be the living Power and prime Agent of all human Perception, and as a repetition in the finite mind

of the eternal act of creation in the infinite I AM. The secondary I consider as an echo of the former, co-existing with the conscious will, yet still as identical with the primary in the *kind* of its agency, and differing only in *degree*, and in the *mode* of its operation. It dissolves, diffuses, dissipates, in order to re-create; or where this process is rendered impossible, yet still at all events it struggles to idealize and to unify. It is essentially *vital*, even as all objects (*as* objects) are essentially fixed and dead. . . .

The poet, described in *ideal* perfection, brings the whole soul of man into activity, with the subordination of its faculties to each other, according to their relative worth and dignity. He diffuses a tone, and spirit of unity, that blends, and (as it were) *fuses*, each into each, by that synthetic and magical power, to which we have exclusively appropriated the name of imagination. This power, first put in action by the will and understanding, . . . reveals itself in the balance or reconciliation of opposite or discordant qualities: of sameness, with difference; of the general, with the concrete; the idea, with the image; the individual, with the representative; the sense of novelty and freshness, with old and familiar objects; a more than usual state of emotion, with more than usual order; judgement ever awake and steady self-possession, with enthusiasm and feeling profound or vehement; . . . .

S.T. Coleridge, *Biographia Literaria* (1817), Vol. 1, pp.295-96; Vol. 2, pp.11-12.

Coleridge is nothing if not myriad-minded, as he himself said of Shakespeare, but behind the complications of his thought we can feel his eager insistence on a creatively active power that causes different entities found in experience to form new artistic wholes. The friendship between Coleridge and Davy lapsed eventually, but both were fascinated by the kind of unitary ideas that made the universe 'a cosmic web, woven by God, and held together by the crossed strands of attractive and repulsive forces' (Williams, *Michael Faraday*, p.64) at the beginning of a century in which electricity was linked with chemical action, magnetism and light, heat with mechanical work and eventually in 1905, mass with energy. Two fertile and creative minds were joined in an enterprise that was visionary as well as practical. Towards the end of his life Davy produced a romantic work called *Consolations in Travel; or, The Last Days of a Philosopher* (1829), where, as John Beer rightly comments, 'questions of influence or confluence . . . shade into one another bewilderingly' (*Coleridge's Poetic Intelligence* (1977), p.284). In Dialogue 5 of this book Davy wrote that the imagination of 'the chemical philosopher' must be 'active and brilliant in seeking analogies; yet entirely under the influence of the judgment in applying them' (Ibid, pp.252-53). He could have been speaking of the Romantic poet, able to make unity out of the diversity of phenomena, through a mind

> . . . creator and receiver both,
> Working but in alliance with the works
> Which it beholds.

> William Wordsworth, *The Prelude* (1805), Book 2,
> ll.273-275.

Meteorology and Natural Description

Adam Walker once wrote of a moonlight excursion on the lake at Keswick with musicians in the boat sounding horns at intervals to awaken the echoes and stimulate the imagination: 'Blest Imagination! . . . Call that Rock a Giant – This, the dread Chimera – That, a Centaur – Make every Mount a Monster; for among the undefined forms that surround us, the mind may mould a new creation (*Remarks Made in a Tour from London to the Lakes*, 1792, pp.102-103). This typical eighteenth-century man of feeling could be more rigorous in his responses to nature, since he was principally a lecturer in science, and 'natural science', Coleridge claimed, 'which commences with the material phaenomenon as the reality and substance of things existing, does yet by the necessity of theorising unconsciously, and as it were instinctively, end in nature as an intelligence; and by this tendency the science of nature becomes finally natural philosophy . . . .' (*Biographia Literaria*, Vol. 1, p.256). Again we realise the unity of culture about the turn of the century; men of taste and sensibility were also 'experimental philosophers', that is, scientists. In Walker's *A System of Familiar Philosophy* (1799) can be found an explanation of the material phenomenon of the 'wild and wonderful harmony' produced by the Aeolian harp (p.270), or theories that 'fire, light, heat, caloric, phlogiston [two hypothetical substances], and electricity' were 'but modifications of one and the same principle' (p.xi). Walker thought of electricity 'as the matter of the sun's atmosphere . . . projected from him into infinite space' towards the earth,

> but as it approaches the lower and more dense part of the atmosphere, it meets increasing resistance, and is often obliged to force its way through the non-conducting lower regions; producing the terrible corruscations and explosions of thunder and lightning. In the clouds it meets with a receptacle (for water admits and conducts electricity), and when those clouds are not over-charged, the air is in peace. . . . When the air is moist, electricity finds an easy passage into the earth, without commotion; and hence the earth has been generally considered as the grand reservoir of it; and from that reservoir we pump it by electric machines and other frictions, being incapable by such means of exciting much from the air. When the rays of electricity, therefore, come the most directly to the earth, as in summer, a greater quantity may be poured on the dry air than it can conduct, and hence the clouds will be in a positive or abundant state, while the earth, comparatively, may be in a negative state; the consequence will be a violent effort to restore equality by a storm of thunder and lightning; and the air near the earth will be found positive and negative by fits, while the storm lasts. When the clouds are scattered at a distance from one another, the lightning is often seen darting from one to another, where the air is too rare or thin to form much resistance to its passage, and we see

lightning without having thunder. . . . the evaporation goes on, water rises through the air, flying on the wings of electricity (for air approaching to a vacuum is a conductor).

Adam Walker, *A System of Familiar Philosophy* (1799), pp.356-58.

We can see that Walker made no attempt to confine himself to a neutral or objective style when teaching the old science, or art, of meteorology (*OED*, 1620). A later section of *A System*, on optics, begins with a cry of aesthetic delight, reminiscent of *Remarks Made in a Tour*, before proceeding to scientific explanation: 'The rainbow is certainly the most beautiful meteor [atmospheric occurrence] in nature. As it never makes its appearance but when a spectator is situated between the sun and a shower of rain, it follows that the sun and drops of rain cause the phaenomenon' (p.429). His enthusiasm and liveliest phrasing, however, are infinitely surpassed when they are juxtaposed with the poems of his most famous pupil, Shelley, in *Prometheus Unbound . . . with Other Poems* (1820, pp.197; 199).

Sublime on the towers of my skiey bowers
    Lightning my pilot sits,
In a cavern under is fettered the thunder,
    Its struggles and howls at fits;

*   *   *

Sunbeam-proof, I hang like a roof,
    The mountains its columns be.
The triumphal arch through which I march
    With hurricane, fire, and snow,
When the powers of the air are chained to my chair,
    Is the million-coloured bow;
The sphere-fire above its soft colours wove,
    Whilst the moist earth was laughing below.

P.B. Shelley, 'The Cloud', ll.17-20; 65-72.

Shelley's interest in science had begun very early in life. One of his sisters wrote, 'My heart would sink with fear at his approach; but shame kept me silent, and, with as many others as he could collect, we were placed hand-in-hand round the nursery table to be electrified' (R. Holmes, *Shelley: The Pursuit* (1974), p.17). Humphry Davy performed similar experiments at the Royal Institution with, one hopes, consenting adults, since his battery had 2000 double plates. In fact, the line between scientist, gentleman amateur and poet was quite indistinct at the turn of the eighteenth century. Desmond King-Hele tells us that Shelley was like Walker in overestimating the role played by atmospheric electricity in cloud formation. In this respect, both were following the standards of the time, but much of Shelley's poetry is scientifically unexceptionable.

> Thou on whose stream, 'mid the steep sky's
>   commotion,
> Loose clouds like earth's decaying leaves are shed,
> Shook from the tangled boughs of Heaven and Ocean,
>
> Angels of rain and lightning: there are spread
> On the blue surface of thine airy surge,
> Like the bright hair uplifted from the head
>
> Of some fierce Maenad, even from the dim verge
> Of the horizon on the zenith's height
> The locks of the approaching storm. Thou dirge
>
> Of the dying year, to which this closing night
> Will be the dome of a vast sepulchre,
> Vaulted with all thy congregated might
> Of vapours, from whose solid atmosphere
> Black rain, and fire, and hail will burst; O hear!
>
>   P.B. Shelley, 'Ode to the West Wind' (1819),
>   stanza 2.

We can compare these lines with the passages from Walker quoted above, or, for a modern view of the 'special scientific flavour' of Shelley's poetry, we can turn to the detailed analysis King-Hele provides in *Shelley: His Thought and Work* (1960). He notes, for example, that clouds 'like earth's decaying leaves' have the shapes of detached fractostratus, which differ very much in appearance from the long plume cirrus clouds, 'Like the bright hair . . . / Of some fierce Maenad', priestess of Bacchus. Such accuracy in depicting clouds in storm conditions was quite novel and was reinforced by the man who first classified cloud types and gave them the Latin names we know, Luke Howard, in 1803. His later book, *The Climate of London* (1818–20), inspired two major painters, Constable and Turner, opening up 'a new vista of artistic perception' (D. King-Hele, pp.215-18).

The Romantic imagination is like the scientific as defined by Davy, 'active and brilliant in seeking analogies'. A stanza in Shelley's 'The Sensitive Plant' is on one level an expression of the subjective experience of a mingling of sense-impressions.

> And the hyacinth purple, and white, and blue,
> Which flung from its bells a sweet peal anew
> Of music so delicate, soft, and intense,
> It was felt like an odour within the sense.

>   P.B. Shelley, 'The Sensitive Plant' (1820), ll.25-28.

On another level, it reflects a mode of scientific thought which strove to link their separate causes in nature. In addition, however, the Romantic imagination was a unifying and symbol-making faculty, as Coleridge went to such pains to explain in the *Biographia Literaria*. Sentient human beings might discover a mystically quiet view of nature, as in Wordsworth's 'Tintern Abbey', or something more active.

> And what if all of animated nature
> Be but organic Harps diversely fram'd,
> That tremble into thought, as o'er them sweeps
> Plastic and vast, one intellectual Breeze,
> At once the Soul of each, and God of all?

>   S.T. Coleridge, 'The Eolian Harp' (1817), ll.44-48.

Shelley found in nature revolutionary symbols. His West Wind is a force, a fierce energy, which can drive his 'dead thoughts over the universe / Like withered leaves to quicken a new birth' ('Ode to the West Wind, ll.63-64). The old image of the breath of life is now reinforced by lightning or electricity, focus of intense scientific speculation and experiment, but for Shelley a symbol of human powers as well, a secular version of the 'sacred spark created by His breath' in Davy's poem.

> The great writers of our own age are, we have reason to suppose, the companions and forerunners of some unimagined change in our social condition or the opinions which cement it. The cloud of mind is discharging its collected lightning, and the equilibrium between institutions and opinions is now restoring, or is about to be restored.

> P.B. Shelley, *Prometheus Unbound* (1820), Preface.

Promethean Powers

The restoration of equilibrium, when human creative powers are truly represented in their social and political institutions, is celebrated in the visionary last act of *Prometheus Unbound A Lyrical Drama* (1820). The 'lightning' of human minds can both animate and reorganise experience – in art ('Through the cold mass / Of Marble and of colour his dreams pass'), in language ('a perpetual orphic song, / Which rules with Daedal harmony a throng / Of thoughts and forms') and in the sciences. As the passage (p.144) continues, ancient symbolic figures like Orpheus, poet and lute-player, and the Athenian inventor and craftsman, Daedalus, are associated with contemporary scientists like Davy and William Herschel, whose great telescope led to the discovery of Uranus, or his son John, who discovered and catalogued hundreds of nebulae and unknown star-clusters.

THE EARTH

The lightning is his slave; heaven's utmost deep
Gives up her stars, and like a flock of sheep
They pass before his eye, are numbered, and roll on!

* * *

As the dissolving warmth of dawn may fold
A half infrozen dew-globe, green, and gold,
And crystalline, till it becomes a winged mist,
And wanders up the vault of the blue day,
Outlives the noon, and on the sun's last ray
Hangs o'er the sea, a fleece of fire and amethyst.

THE MOON

Thou art folded, thou art lying
In the light which is undying
Of thine own joy, and heaven's smile divine;
All suns and constellations shower
On thee a light, a life, a power
Which doth array thy sphere; thou pourest thine
On mine, on mine!

P.B. Shelley, *Prometheus Unbound* (1820), Act IV,
ll.412-420; 431-443.

This wholly lyrical last act presents the millenium, a new heaven and a new earth. We should recall the *'Life, Power, Being'* which Coleridge felt was suffused throughout the cosmos. More particularly, we can refer to Walker's scientific assertion that electricity is 'matter of the sun's atmosphere' and his general theory that light is 'fire itself, originally emanating from the sun and fixed stars, . . . being repulsed radiantly in all directions' (*A System*, p.393). In ordinary human perception, the sun appears to be 'a round Disk of fire somewhat like a Guinea', a coin, but to one poet of the time it appeared to be 'an Innumerable company of the Heavenly host crying "Holy Holy Holy is the Lord God Almighty"'. Angela Leighton, who cites these lines from Blake's *Vision of the Last Judgment*, traces Shelley's comparable view of human potential in *Prometheus Unbound* – through a poetic creativity 'like veiled lightning asleep', beyond a vision 'blinded / By the white lightning', and on to the triumphant 'liberation of the human mind's imaginings from despair' celebrated in the last act (*Shelley and the Sublime*, (1984), pp.15; 92-99). A firm structure of scientific thought helps organise and make more subtle Shelley's final symbolic imagery of the earth, on which 'suns and constellations shower . . . / a light, a life, a power'. He is not restricted to the simple choice between outer sight and inward vision. Walker provides the idea of a state of equilibrium, attained after 'a violent effort to restore equality'. Then human powers and cosmic forces become 'modifications of one and the same principle'. The new earth is metaphorically irradiated and irradiating, bathed in the undying light of its 'own joy, and heaven's smile divine'. At the end of an early poem Shelley had expressed himself more plainly.

> Happiness
> And science dawn, though late, upon the earth; . . .
> Whilst every shape and mode of matter lends
> Its force to the omnipotence of mind.

P.B. Shelley, *Queen Mab* (1813), VIII, ll.227-228; 235-236.

Shelley found in contemporary science an explanation of natural energies in man and nature that could be assimilated with his optimistic revision of the myth of Prometheus, who had stolen fire from the gods for the sake of humanity. Mary Shelley's *Frankenstein; or, the Modern Prometheus* (1818), written when she was about nineteen, might be regarded as an anticipatory parody of her husband's *Prometheus Unbound* (1820), its basic values are so radically opposed. It is a very different version of the myth of Prometheus, in his role as creator rather than as rebel.

Her introduction to the 1831 edition specifies the scientific intention as she recalls her planning: 'Perhaps a corpse would be re-animated; galvanism had given token of such things; perhaps the component parts of a creature might be manufactured, brought together, and endued with vital warmth' (p.x). 'Galvanism' (*OED*, 1797) is a reference to the experiments performed in the 1780s by Luigi Galvani, who induced muscular spasms in the nerves of dissected frogs by applying electricity. There is no need to be more precise, for some of the extraordinary popular success of *Frankenstein* probably arises from the bold simplicity of its 'science'.

> I collected the instruments of life around me, that I
> might infuse a spark of being into the lifeless thing that
> lay at my feet. It was already one in the morning; the
> rain pattered dismally against the panes, and my candle
> was nearly burnt out, when, by the glimmer of the
> half-extinguished light, I saw the dull yellow eye of the
> creature open; it breathed hard, and a convulsive
> motion agitated its limbs.

> Mary Shelley, *Frankenstein* (1818), Chapter 5, p.43.

Precise scientific allusions have to be scraped together in the
book as a whole, though the general background is clear
enough. A passage with notes in Erasmus Darwin's *Botanic
Garden* (1791, pp.19-20), including lines on a mythical lyre in
the temple of Memnon that sounded when the sun shone on it
('Touch'd by his orient beam, responsive rings / The living
lyre, and vibrates all it's strings'), contains a cluster of
references to natural luminous and electrical phenomena: the
ignis fatuus, the glow-worm, the 'dread Gymnotus' and the
torpedo. The last two are living creatures that can give
electric shocks, eels and rays. Nobody knew how, for despite
the analogies with electricity, 'neither spark nor any other
indication of electrical tension could be detected in them.'

> The benumbing effect of the torpedo had been
> ascertained to depend on certain singularly constructed
> organs composed of membranous columns, filled from
> end to end with laminae [thin plates], separated from
> each other by a fluid: but of its mode of action no
> satisfactory account could be given; .... . But the pile
> of Volta supplied at once the analogies both of structure
> and of effect, so as to leave little doubt of the electrical
> nature of the apparatus, or of the power, a most
> wonderful one certainly, of the animal, to determine,
> by an effort of its will, that concurrence of conditions
> on which its activity depends. This remained, as it
> probably ever will remain, mysterious and inexplicable;
> but the principle once established, that there exists in
> the animal economy a power of determining the

developement of electric excitement, capable of being transmitted along the nerves, . . . it became an easy step . . . to look to the brain, a wonderfully constituted organ, for which no mode of action possessing the least plausibility had ever been devised, as the source of the required electrical power.

> John Herschel, *A Preliminary Discourse on the Study of Natural Philosophy* (1831), 1832 edn, pp.342-43.

Mary Shelley cut through the complexity of analogy and speculation by straightforwardly making electricity the life force. Her aim was more psychological than metaphysical. Despite its creaking contrivances, its exploitation of Gothic awe and terror, its sublime settings and resonating landscapes, *Frankenstein* is a book about a nineteenth-century scientist, creating by means then impossible but *not* supernatural a monster. This monster became his affliction, almost his other self, and within a score of years it had assumed his name, at least in popular legend. Frankenstein is the new Promethean scientist, not his monstrous creature. Mary Shelley is far more convincing in her treatment of character than she is about the scientific matters involved. She anticipates the heightened prose realism of the Victorian novel in Frankenstein's thirst for knowledge, his obsession with the mystery of life, his combined pity and terror when he only succeeds in creating a monster, not to mention the plausibility within the terms of a strictly marvellous plot of that monster's gradual awakening to the world of sense-impressions, language, sex and human culture. The novels of Emily Brontë, Dickens and Wilkie Collins are yet to come. More important perhaps is the fact that a young woman, trying to think of a ghost story in friendly rivalry with her husband and Byron during days when, she tells us, 'death and grief were but words, which found no true echo in my heart' (*Frankenstein*, 1831 edn, p.xii), had unexpectedly made a literary discovery that ran counter to almost all we have so far seen in Romanticism – the power of modern science to create human desolation. Her theme of perilous scientific interference with the fundamental mysteries of life makes *Frankenstein* the prototype of numerous works of science fiction.

Science Fantasy

Davy's discovery of silicon is sufficient in itself to show the long-term importance of basic research, but the discoveries of Michael Faraday in the course of a long career devoted to experiments and theorising were, like Davy's invention of the safety lamp, of immediate practical value. To him we owe our electric motors, transformers and dynamos. No mathematician, he thought in a very concrete manner. 'You can hardly imagine', he wrote in 1845, 'how I am struggling to exert my poetical ideas just now for the discovery of analogies and remote figures respecting the earth, sun, and all sorts of things – for I think that is the true way (corrected by judgment) to work out a discovery' (Williams, *Michael Faraday*, p.443). Not only is his habit of speculative thought like that of Davy, he adroitly developed a similar pattern of concepts. In paragraph 2146 of his sequentially numbered *Experimental Researches*, Faraday claimed that 'the various forms under which the forces of matter are made manifest have one common origin; or, in other words, are so directly related and mutually dependent, that they are convertible, as it were, one into another, and possess equivalents of power in their action.' He found an analogy between a magnet, 'a voltaic battery immersed in water or any other electrolyte [solution that conducts electricity]', and çertain living things, 'a gymnotus . . . or torpedo, at the moment when these creatures, at their own will, fill the surrounding fluid with lines of electric force' (paragraph 3276). The lines of force depend on the existence of a *medium*, water or electrolyte, so a magnet must operate in the same way, he argued. Its energy must lie in the medium through which the magnetic lines of force pass, not in the magnet by itself. 'This was the fundamental concept of classical field theory', L.P. Williams comments (*Michael Faraday*, p.452). These theories of the electromagnetic field, developed by Maxwell, brought about the greatest change in our conception of physical reality since Newton, according to

Einstein (*James Clerk Maxwell: A Commemoration Volume 1831–1931* (1931), pp.66-67).

Amongst the prolific writings of Edward Bulwer-Lytton, which include historical romances, novels of high and of low society and fiction of the occult, is a science fantasy called *The Coming Race*. An American discovers in the depths of the earth an unknown country: a wonderfully advanced people without war, crime, poverty, sex discrimination or creative literature: women taller, stronger, cleverer and more ardent in wooing, 'which perhaps forms the secret motive of most lady asserters of women rights above ground': innocently luxurious houses in which every room 'has its mechanical contrivances for melodious sounds, usually tuned down to soft-murmured notes' (pp.76; 115). This Swiftian satire, which has amongst its manifold concerns the evolution of language (Chapter 12) and of skull types (Chapter 15), actually quotes Faraday's paragraph 2146, since every aspect of the apparently utopian existence of the dwellers underground depends upon 'the latent powers stored in the all-permeating fluid which they denominate Vril' (p.58). A character says to the wondering American,

> I should call it electricity, except that it comprehends in its manifold branches other forces of nature, to which, in our scientific nomenclature, differing names are assigned, such as magnetism, galvanism, &c. These people consider that in vril they have arrived at the unity in natural energetic agencies, which has been conjectured by many philosophers above ground, and which Faraday ... intimates under the more cautious term of correlation .... These subterranean philosophers assert that by one operation of vril, which Faraday would perhaps call 'atmospheric magnetism', they can influence the variations of temperature – in plain words, the weather; that by other operations, akin to those ascribed to mesmerism, electro-biology, odic force [another hypothetical force invented by a German thinker], &c., but applied scientifically through vril conductors, they can exercise influence over minds, and bodies animal and vegetable, to an extent not surpassed

in the romances of our mystics. To all such agencies
they give the common name of vril.

E. Bulwer-Lytton, *The Coming Race* (1871),
Chapter 7, pp.47-48.

Bulwer cleverly manipulates his borrowed idea of the
correlation, or convertibility, of natural forces, achieving some
very fair predictions in a general way – universal electric
lighting, individual flight, electric shock treatment, laser-like
weapons and remote control of robots.

> She set complicated pieces of machinery into
> movement, arrested the movement or continued it,
> until, within an incredibly short time, various kinds of
> raw material were reproduced as symmetrical works of
> art, complete and perfect. . . . '. . . no form of matter is
> motionless and inert: every particle is constantly in
> motion and constantly acted on by agencies, of which
> heat is the most apparent and rapid, but vril the most
> subtle, and, when skilfully wielded, the most powerful.
> So that, in fact, the current launched by my hand and
> guided by my will does but render quicker and more
> potent the action which is eternally at work upon every
> particle of matter, however inert and stubborn it may
> seem. . . . Without this we could not make our
> automata supply the place of servants.'

Ibid., Chapter 16, pp.129-30; 132-33.

Tempting as it is to luxuriate in the fanciful details, we should
not forget the imaginative breadth of the fundamental
conception, which, when Faraday applied it to the
'atmospheric magnetism' Bulwer mentioned, led to a 'vision of
the earth, wrapped snugly in its lines of magnetic force. To
disturb one was to disturb them all just as brushing a spider's
web sent a tremor through all the strands' (Williams, *Michael
Faraday*, p.402). The point is exceptionally important, for we
might otherwise miss the literary relevance of revolutionary
ideas of a major kind about the nature of physical reality. Few

authors make such direct allusions and salient use of scientific concepts as Bulwer does, in a manifest 'science fantasy'.

The novels of Dickens are often neglected in this context, despite a pioneering article by Ann Y. Wilkinson, '*Bleak House*: From Faraday to Judgment Day' (*Journal of English Literary History*, Vol. 34, 1967, pp.225-47). *Bleak House* (1852–53) contains one definite episode of a scientific nature, the death by 'spontaneous combustion' of Mr Krook: 'And the burning smell is there – and the soot is there, and the oil is there – and he is not there!' (Chapter 32). Dickens obstinately defended this physiological impossibility in the preface but Ann Wilkinson is able to show how Dickens drew upon articles he himself had commissioned for two issues of his popular periodical *Household Words* (3 August and 7 September 1850), based on Faraday's notes for one of his famous lecture-demonstrations to children, 'The Chemical History of a Candle'. The second article, 'The Laboratory in the Chest', rather fancifully evokes a 'Young Davy', who turns Faraday's parallel between chemical combustion and human respiration – we take in oxygen, evolve heat and exhale carbonic acid – into a ridiculous conclusion that 'great spirit drinkers' may have 'a system' that is 'too inflammable'. The scientific instance, in article and novel, is worthless in itself, but Dickens makes it clear that the death of the mock Lord Chancellor, Krook, 'inborn, inbred, engendered in the corrupted humours of the vicious body itself', is meant to stand for the coming end of 'all Lord Chancellors in all Courts, and of all authorities in all places under all names soever' (*Bleak House*, Chapter 32). *Bleak House*, it is shown, is organised as a set of interlocking systems – Chancery, Parliament, Industry, the Aristocracy, Philanthropy, even the world itself – which are in their rubbishy chaos ready for explosion or death by pollution.

> Darkness rests upon Tom-all-Alone's. Dilating and dilating since the sun went down last night, it has gradually swelled until it fills every void in the place. For a time there were some dungeon lights burning as the lamp of Life burns in Tom-all-Alone's, heavily, heavily, in the nauseous air, and winking – as that lamp,

too, winks in Tom-all-Alone's – at many horrible things. But they are blotted out. The moon has eyed Tom with a dull cold stare, as admitting some puny emulation of herself in his desert region unfit for life and blasted by volcanic fires, but she has passed on, and is gone. The blackest nightmare in the infernal stables grazes on Tom-all-Alone's, and Tom is fast asleep.

Much mighty speech-making there has been, both in and out of Parliament, concerning Tom, and much wrathful disputation how Tom shall be got right. Whether he shall be put into the main road by constables, or by beadles, or by bellringing, or by force of figures, or by correct principles of taste, or by high church, or by low church, or by no church; whether he shall be set to splitting trusses of polemical straws with the crooked knife of his mind, or whether he shall be put to stone-breaking instead. In the midst of which dust and noise, there is but one thing perfectly clear, to wit, that Tom only may and can, or shall and will, be reclaimed according to somebody's theory but nobody's practice. And in the hopeful meantime, Tom goes to perdition head foremost in his old determined spirit.

But he has his revenge. Even the winds are his messengers, and they serve him in these hours of darkness. There is not a drop of Tom's corrupted blood but propagates infection and contagion somewhere. It shall pollute, this very night, the choice stream (in which chemists on analysis would find the genuine nobility) of a Norman house, and his Grace shall not be able to say Nay to the infamous alliance. There is not an atom of Tom's slime, not a cubic inch of any pestilential gas in which he lives, not one obscenity or degradation about him, not an ignorance, not a wickedness, not a brutality of his committing, but shall work in retribution, through every order of society, ...

Charles Dickens, *Bleak House* (1852–53),
Chapter 46, ed. N. Page (1971), pp.682-83.

Dickens' interrelated metaphors, drawn from chemistry, astronomy, physiology and medicine, are correlated with the various agencies of social control, from police forces to churches and schools, even in three short paragraphs. Ann Wilkinson's analysis of this long and complex novel demonstrates that *Bleak House* has 'physical laws which are almost exact analogues of moral laws'; its social and human systems are composed of disordered forces like those of the court of Chancery, 'seen in the newer, larger, infinitely disquieting perspective of a universe where there are, for example, circular lines of force that create fields of influence around a magnetic centre' (*'Bleak House*: From Faraday to Judgment Day', p.229). To see Chancery as the legal *medium* in which 'decaying houses', 'blighted lands', a 'worn-out lunatic in every madhouse' and numerous characters are helplessly caught is not difficult, nor can we fail to see that it is representative in the formal organisation of the novel. But to appreciate Dickens' more intuitive grasp of other great generalisations of the time, the laws of thermodynamics (heat-power), requires commentary that goes beyond explanation of a candle's burning.

Thermodynamics and the Promised End

Ann Wilkinson contends that the laws of thermodynamics 'give modern specificity and focus to myth, to the ancient myth of the death of the sun' (Ibid, p.247). We might begin by noting that Carlyle had just given a more modern turn to that myth when he described the 19th century as a 'waste-weltering epoch . . . in the wild dim-lighted chaos all stars of Heaven gone out'.

> No star of Heaven visible, hardly now to any man; the pestiferous fogs, and foul exhalations grown continual, have, except on the highest mountain-tops, blotted out all stars: will-o'-wisps, of various course and colour, take the place of stars. Over the wild-surging chaos, in the leaden air, are only sudden glares of revolutionary lightning; then mere darkness, with philanthropistic

phosphorescences, empty meteoric lights; here and there an ecclesiastical luminary still hovering, hanging on to its old quaking fixtures, pretending still to be a Moon or Sun, – though visibly it is but a Chinese Lantern made of *paper* mainly, with candle-end foully dying in the heart of it.

Thomas Carlyle, Life of John Sterling (1851), Chapter 5, p.51.

Carlyle influenced every writer of the age, including scientists like John Tyndall and T.H. Huxley as well as Dickens, but where his metaphors in this passage are not drawn from industry or commerce, they look backwards to the Romantic writing we have just examined.

Thermodynamics deals with transference of energy and is a branch of science developed in the mid-nineteenth century. In 1847 Hermann Helmholtz proposed a law of 'the conservation of living force', later called 'the conservation of energy'. He contended that in any given system energy is always preserved in some form. If a force in nature is exhausted in operation, another force gains the power lost. Thus the watch and the crossbow are both wound by the force of a living arm, so that they then possess a mechanical power held in reserve until released, slowly or quickly as the case may be. Even then the energy is not lost ('*how could* it perish?'), for it is converted into heat in some form. In the 1840s too J.P. Joule of Manchester proved that heat could be produced by friction in exact, measurable equivalence to the power expended. The science of thermodynamics therefore studies heat as a form of energy which can be precisely related to other forms – mechanical, chemical, electrical and, in our day, nuclear. The first law of thermodynamics states that energy is neither gained nor lost in operation, only transformed into some equivalent form. The energy of the whole system remains constant. (In special relativity, mass and energy are conserved together.)

But this first law is accompanied by an odious twin, the second law of thermodynamics, which proclaims the ultimate exhaustion of *useful* energy. Mechanical work may produce an exact equivalent in heat, but not the reverse. Heat is one-directional in nature. It passes from a warmer to a colder body without difficulty, but to make a cold body colder, more energy has to be expended than is actually gained. If the second law is applied to the known universe as a whole, we are presented with a scientific image of the promised end, the horror of an earth unfit for human life.

> The object of the present communication is to call attention to the remarkable consequences which follow from [S.] Carnot's proposition, that there is an absolute waste of mechanical energy available to man when heat is allowed to pass from one body to another at a lower temperature, ... As it is most certain that Creative Power alone can either call into existence or annihilate mechanical energy, the 'waste' referred to cannot be annihilation, but must be some transformation of energy. . . .
>
> 1. There is at present in the material world a universal tendency to the dissipation of mechanical energy.
> 2. Any *restoration* of mechanical energy, without more than an equivalent of dissipation, is impossible in inanimate material processes, and is probably never affected by means of organized matter, either endowed with vegetable life or subjected to the will of an animated creature.
> 3. Within a finite period of time past the earth must have been, and within a finite period of time to come the earth must again be, unfit for the habitation of man as at present constituted, unless operations have been, or are to be performed, which are impossible under the laws to which the known operations going on at present in the material world are subject.

> William Thomson (later Lord Kelvin), 'On a Universal Tendency in Nature to the Dissipation of Mechanical Energy', *Philosophical Magazine*, October 1852, pp.304; 306.

Here is the so-called 'heat-death of the universe', the end of organic life through irreversible physical processes. It is sometimes expressed through the concept of 'entropy',

Clausius's measure of the *un*availability of thermal energy in a system. By the second law of thermodynamics entropy never decreases. Alternatively, one may say that disorder never decreases, since heat at higher temperatures may be regarded as energy of a higher degree of order and heat at lower temperatures does not of its own accord rise to a higher state. Time's arrow has a definite direction in thermodynamical terms.

In the middle years of the nineteenth century physical scientists were bringing about major shifts in our understanding, from ideas of an essential unity of forces in nature towards the convertibility of energy in a closed system. Maxwell thought that Mrs Somerville's *On the Connexion of the Physical Sciences* (1834), with its eight revised and up-dated editions between 1834 and 1849, showed that 'there existed a widespread desire to be able to form some notion of physical science as a whole'. Her unity, however, was of scientific method rather than of processes in nature. With regard to 'the shaping of the concept of the conservation of energy' during this period, W.R. Grove's 'Correlation of Physical Forces' (1842) was in his view just the sort of popular essay that could diffuse ideas through the general culture of the age (*Nature*, 20 August 1874). The dramatic, if distant, consequences of the second law of thermodynamics first announced by Kelvin in April 1852, and developed in other scientific papers of the 1850s, attracted little attention (J.D. Burchfield, *Lord Kelvin and the Age of the Earth* (1975), pp.23; 26), but it is possible that Dickens with his extraordinary powers of assimilation may have broached something like this theme in the first paragraph of *Bleak House* with his allusion to flakes of London soot 'as big as full-grown snow-flakes – gone into mourning, one might imagine, for the death of the sun'. In the years to come it became common intellectual currency in Kelvin's form. His article 'On the Age of the Sun's Heat' (*Macmillan's Magazine*, March 1862), again suggesting a future of a few millions of years, had a tremendous impact. A measure of the human and literary response can be seen if lines from Maxwell's 'A Paradoxical Ode' of 1878 are allowed to follow Shelley's lines from *Prometheus Unbound* (1820, Act IV, ll.153-58, p.131).

And our singing shall build
In the void's loose field
A world for the Spirit of Wisdom to wield;
  We will take our plan
  From the new world of man,
And our work shall be called the Promethean.

Till in the twilight of the Gods
When earth and sun are frozen clods,
With all its energy degraded,
Matter to ether shall have faded;
We, that is, all the work we've done
As waves in ether shall for ever run
In ever widening spheres through heavens beyond the
  sun.

> Quoted in *James Clerk Maxwell: A Commemo-*
> *ration Volume 1831–1931*, p.5.

Maxwell is here referring, not too seriously perhaps, to what
Darwin about 1876 had called 'the view now held by most
physicists, namely that the sun with all the planets will in time
grow too cold for life, unless indeed some great body dashes
into the sun and thus gives it fresh life' (*Charles Darwin,
Thomas Henry Huxley: Autobiographies*, ed. Gavin de Beer
(1974), p.53).

It is in H.G. Wells' *The Time Machine* that we find the
clearest literary illustration of the *Götterdämmerung*, the
mythical twilight of the gods, and all other organic life. His
time traveller tells of a voyage into the remote future.

'So I travelled, stopping ever and again, in great
strides of a thousand years or more, drawn on by the
mystery of the earth's fate, watching with a strange
fascination the sun grow larger and duller in the
westward sky, and the life of the old earth ebb away. At
last, more than thirty million years hence, the huge
red-hot dome of the sun had come to obscure nearly a
tenth part of the darkling heavens. Then I stopped once
more, for the crawling multitude of crabs had

disappeared, and the red beach, save for its livid green liverworts and lichens, seemed lifeless. And now it was flecked with white. A bitter cold assailed me. . . .'

'The darkness grew apace; a cold wind began to blow in freshening gusts from the east, and the showering white flakes in the air increased in number. From the edge of the sea came a ripple and whisper. Beyond these lifeless sounds the world was silent. Silent? It would be hard to convey the stillness of it. All the sounds of man, the bleating of sheep, the cries of birds, the hum of insects, the stir that makes the background of our lives – all that was over. As the darkness thickened, the eddying flakes grew more abundant, dancing before my eyes; and the cold of the air more intense. At last, one by one, swiftly, one after the other, the white peaks of the distant hills vanished into blackness. The breeze rose to a moaning wind. I saw the black central shadow of the eclipse sweeping towards me. In another moment the pale stars alone were visible. All else was rayless obscurity. The sky was absolutely black.

Chapter 13, *The New Review*, Vol. 12, 1895,
pp.581-82.

In thus envisaging the imminent end of the world Wells is in effect reviving the cosmic determinism of Laplace, whose *Essai Philosophique sur les Probabilités* (1814) contains the famous assertion that the present state of the physical universe is the effect of its past state and the cause of the one to follow, so that an intelligence in possession of all the data and great enough to analyse it would both know past and future with perfect certainty. He repeated it in his *Mécanique Céleste*, which explains A.H. Clough's sarcastic lines.

Earth goes by chemic forces; Heaven's
A Mécanique Céleste!
And heart and mind of human kind
A watch-work as the rest!

A.H. Clough 'The New Sinai', *Ambarvalia* (1849),
ll.55-58.

Nobody then knew of radioactivity, only discovered in 1896 and therefore not included in calculations of the age of the earth, nor of the nuclear reactions in the sun that would greatly extend Kelvin's estimates. But Wells is not really interested in the details once he has set his time machine in motion. Given his celestial mechanism by the nineteenth-century physicists, he joins poets from Sidney to Dylan Thomas in raging against the dying of the light and anything that will make the much-loved earth unlovely and unloved.

The Scientific Love of Beauty

Response to the world of sense-impressions generally is both detailed and passionate in writers of the nineteenth century, some obviously impressed by the methods of science and yet wishing to merge them with more traditional concerns. John Ruskin, admirer of Turner, is a key figure.

> Nor is it even just to speak of the love of beauty as in all respects unscientific; for there is a science of the aspects of things, as well as of their nature; and it is as much a fact to be noted in their constitution, that they produce such and such an effect upon the eye and heart (as, for instance, the minor scales of sound cause melancholy), as that they are made up of certain atoms or vibrations of matter.

> John Ruskin, *Modern Painters*, Vol. 3 (1856), Chapter 17, para. 43.

Beauty and emotion combined, however, should not produce sentimentality; the eye must be fixed firmly on the object in all its particularity, with a sharp awareness of its dynamic context in time and place. A virtuoso command of language is required to catch the skies or water in motion or to realise the affinities and complicated organisation of visual phenomena. When the world experienced extraordinary sunsets after the volcanic eruption at Krakatoa, for instance, a number of letters were sent to the scientific periodical *Nature*. Two of them were written by the poet Gerard Manley Hopkins, displaying all the sensitivity, exactitude and verbal facility one might expect of him.

> A sun seen as green or blue for hours together is a phenomenon only witnessed after the late Krakatoa eruptions . . . but a sun which turns green or blue just at setting is, I believe, an old and, we may say, ordinary one, little remarked till lately. . . . It is, possibly, an optical effect only, due to a reaction (from the red or yellow sunset light, to its complementary colour) taking place in the overstrained eye at the moment when the light is suddenly cut off, either by the sun's disappearance or by his entering a much thicker belt of vapour, which, foreshortened as the vapour is close to the horizon, may happen almost instantaneously. And this is confirmed by a kindred phenomenon of sunset. If a very clear, unclouded sun is then gazed at, it often appears not convex, but hollow; swimming – like looking down into a boiling pot or a swinging pail, or into a bowl of quicksilver shaken; and of a lustrous but indistinct blue.
>
> *Nature*, 30 October 1884, p.633.

He knew, it would seem, of Newton's theory of compound colours and 'the opinion that every colour has its complementary colour, with which when mixed it gives white' (*Philosophical Magazine*, April 1854, p.254). A similar scientific interest can be found in his poetry.

> Whereas did air not make
> This bath of blue and slake
> His fire, the sun would shake,
> A blear and blinding ball
> With blackness bound, ...
>
> Gerard Manley Hopkins, 'The Blessed Virgin compared to the Air we Breathe', ll.94-98.

But such lines go beyond description of visual phenomena. They explain what might be, what has in fact never been seen till space voyaging in this century: 'Space diverse, systems manifold to see / Revealed by thought alone' (Boole, *Sonnet to the Number Three*).

Hopkins' major poem 'That Nature is a Heraclitean Fire and of the comfort of the Resurrection' begins with a Shelleyan cloudscape.

> Cloud-puffball, torn tufts, tossed pillows | flaunt forth,
>   then chevy on an air-
>   built thoroughfare: heaven-roysterers, in gay-
>   gangs | they throng; . . . .

By line 9 his imagery is used to symbolise a scientific concept, that reality consists of one basic element in a state of flux: 'Million-fuelèd, / nature's bonfire burns on.' Hopkins has here taken us back to what is regarded as the very beginnings of scientific thought in Europe, to the Greek philosopher Heraclitus in the sixth century BC, who gnomically asserted that 'we step and do not step into the same rivers, we exist and do not exist'; and that 'all things are an exchange for fire, and fire for all things' (Sambursky, pp.46-47). Fundamental physical concepts require a descriptive language of symbols, even though they may have to express invisible entities. The ancient Greek model of atoms like tiny, solid balls, for instance, became popular again in the mid-nineteenth century, but Maxwell objected to this concept because it failed to account for 'the vibrations of a molecule as revealed by the spectroscope'. He preferred the explanatory model of Helmholtz and Kelvin, which conceived of atoms as spiralling movements, 'vortex rings', in a perfect fluid, with 'no other properties than inertia, invariable density, and perfect mobility' – in other words, the ether. If two such vortex atoms clashed, they would encounter each other with the lively elasticity of smoke-rings meeting in air (*Encyclopaedia Britannica*, 9th edn, Vol. 3 (1875), 'Atom', p.45). With more emphasis on the means of expression such content becomes 'literary' in the most obvious ways, as Maxwell himself demonstrates in 'A Tyndallic Ode'.

I come from empyrean fires –
  From microscopic spaces,
Where molecules with fierce desires,
  Shiver in hot embraces.
The atoms clash, the spectra flash,
  Projected on the screen,
The double D, magnesian *b*,
  And Thallium's living green.

J. Clerk Maxwell, 'To the Chief Musician upon Nabla',
stanza 2, quoted in *Poems of Science*, eds J. Heath-
Stubbs and Phillips Salman (1984), p.229.

During the whole of the nineteenth century ideas about the
sub-microscopic world of atom and molecule were what they
always had been, unproved hypotheses. 'It is fascinating to
recall that in 1900 outstanding physicists and chemists like
Ernst Mach and Wilhelm Ostwald did not believe in the
existence of atoms' (John Marks, *Science and the Making of the
Modern World* (1983), p.241). Scientists began to believe that
they might actually exist after J.J. Thomson's discovery in 1897
of an even tinier particle, the electron, but it was not until 1911
that Rutherford suggested the possible existence of the
nucleus. Well before this, however, Maxwell had been only too
willing to invent his own theoretical model of electric particles
in operation to account for the known electromagnetic
phenomena. 'I do not bring it forward as a mode of connection
existing in nature', he disarmingly admitted, 'or even as that
which I would willingly assent to as an electrical hypothesis. It
is, however, a mode of connection which is mechanically
conceivable, and easily investigated, ...' (*Scientific Papers*,
(1890), Vol. 1, p.486). It is, in other words, a useful fiction, an
imaginative attempt to anticipate some future, more refined
revelation of physical truth. In an article on 'Theories of
Science and Romance, 1870–1920' Alexander Welsh
demonstrates how these decades were 'critical for the attitude
toward scientific fictions – as they would appear to have been
for literary fictions' (*Victorian Studies*, Vol. 17, 1973–74,
p.139). To think in terms of 'patterns of possible experiences'
rather than 'copies of actual experience' frees scientific

theorising at a time when, for example, competing wave and particle theories of light could each account for only a portion of the experimental data and liberates the novel form in particular from the demands of documentary realism. It can return to the older belief, kept alive in the nineteenth century by authors like Thackeray, that art is a way of probing and assessing reality, not just transcribing it. But there is only meagre evidence that 'the reaction against realism in literature and the new understanding of models in science were changes in thinking about fiction that directly influenced each other' (Welsh, *Victorian Studies*, Vol. 17, 1973–74, p.148).

Kelvin and Maxwell were 'almost nonchalant' about the exact status of their abstractions but they still subjected them to strict mathematical treatment and experimental testing. They could not have agreed with the wittiest, but also the sharpest, literary theorist of this habit of mind amongst their contemporaries.

> Where, if not from the Impressionists, do we get those wonderful brown fogs that come creeping down our streets, blurring the gas-lamps and changing the houses into monstrous shadows? To whom, if not to them and their master [Turner], do we owe the lovely silver mists that brood over our river, and turn to faint forms of fading grace curved bridge and swaying barge? The extraordinary change that has taken place in the climate of London during the last ten years is entirely due to a particular school of Art. You smile. Consider the matter from a scientific or a metaphysical point of view, and you will find that I am right. For what is Nature? Nature is no great mother who has borne us. She is our creation. It is in our brain that she quickens to life. Things are because we see them, and what we see, and how we see it, depends on the Arts that have influenced us. To look at a thing is very different from seeing a thing. One does not see anything until one sees its beauty. Then, and then only, does it come into existence.
>
> Oscar Wilde, 'The Decay of Lying', *Intentions*
> (1891), 1911 edn, pp.38-39.

This may sound similar to Oliver Lodge on the vortex atom: 'It is not yet proved to be true, but is it not highly beautiful? a theory about which one may almost dare to say that it deserves to be true' ('The Ether and Its Functions', *Nature*, 1 February 1883, p.329). But where Lodge hoped for confirmation in reality, it is far from certain that Wilde could have accepted the sublime simplicity of 'Beauty is truth, truth beauty'. 'I wish the Channel,' he continued in this dialogue, 'especially at Hastings, did not look quite so often like a Henry Moore, grey pearl with yellow lights, but then, when Art is more varied, Nature will, no doubt, be more varied also' (Wilde, 'The Decay of Lying, p.41).

The Ultimate Realities

In D.M. Knight's most valuable collection of *Classical Scientific Papers: Chemistry – Second Series* (1970) is a section on 'radiant matter'. In one of his early lectures, given in 1819, Faraday had speculated that there might be four states of matter, solid, liquid, gaseous and 'radiant', though the actual existence of the latter could not be directly shown. Some sixty years later William Crookes, discoverer of thallium and a gifted experimentalist, revived this suggestion as a way of explaining the rays he had discovered proceeding from the cathode in a highly evacuated glass tube. His lectures on the subject are uncompromisingly technical, accompanied by spectacular demonstrations and perhaps 'too florid for the modern taste', Knight suggests, 'but the descriptions are vivid and the generalisations bold' (pp.71-72). The conclusion of a lecture he delivered to the British Association at Sheffield is suffused with that idealism the Victorians regarded as peculiarly poetic.

> In studying this fourth state of matter we seem at length to have within our grasp and obedient to our control the little indivisible particles which with good warrant are supposed to constitute the physical basis of the universe. We have seen that in some of its properties

radiant matter is as material as this table, whilst in other properties it almost assumes the character of radiant energy. We have actually touched the borderland where matter and force seem to merge into one another, the shadowy realm between Known and the Unknown which for me has always had particular temptations. I venture to think that the greatest scientific problems of the future will find their solution in this Border Land, and even beyond; here, it seems to me, lie Ultimate Realities, subtle, far-reaching, wonderful.

Nature, 4 September 1879, pp.439-40.

This most un-nonchalant prose concludes with the falling rhythms of Tennyson's *Morte d'Arthur*,

> But ere he dipt the surface, rose an arm
> Clothed in white samite, mystic, wonderful . . .

Lord Tennyson, *Morte d'Arthur* (1842), ll.143-144.

At the very least he shares with Tennyson a sense of the numinous and even a concept of its geography, most clearly seen in the later version published as one of the Idylls of the King, *The Passing of Arthur*.

> 'He passes to be King among the dead,
> And after healing of his grievous wound
> He comes again; . . .'

*   *   *

> Then from the dawn it seemed there came, but faint
> As from beyond the limit of the world,
> Like the last echo born of a great cry,
> Sounds, as if some fair city were one voice
> Around a king returning from the wars.

Lord Tennyson, *The Passing of Arthur* (1869),
ll.449-51; 457-61.

For Crookes, the physical scientist was on a voyage of discovery.

> As for myself I hold the firm conviction that unflagging research will be rewarded by an insight into natural mysteries such as now can scarcely be conceived. Difficulties, said a keen old statesman, are things to be overcome, and to my thinking Science should disdain the notion of Finality. There is no stopping half-way, and we are resistlessly driven to ceaseless inquiry by the spirit 'That impels all thinking things, all objects of all thought, and rolls through all things.'
>
> *Chemical News*, 6 March 1891; quoted by D.M. Knight in *Classical Scientific Papers: Chemistry 2*, p.123.

The quotation from Wordsworth's 'Tintern Abbey' takes us back to the Romantic unity in diversity with which we began, but the refusal of Crookes to rest content in 'the notion of Finality' reflects his scientific intuition, or judgement, that fundamental discoveries had hardly begun. He was right. His 'radiant matter', the rays, turned out to be streams of electrons, and we have already touched in the introduction on that decline in scientific certainty so characteristic of the twentieth century. For laws with almost scriptural authority are substituted approximations, statistical truths, competing theories and hypotheses, disposable models, experimental margins of error and indeterminacies of many kinds. The image of a voyage into the unknown, with keen-eyed sailors gazing into the mists, is hardly adequate, though a religious poet like Francis Thompson could retain his belief:

> O World invisible, we view thee,
> O World intangible, we touch thee,
> O World unknowable, we know thee . . . !

Francis Thompson, 'In No Strange Land', (c. 1902) ll.1-3.

But a short story by H.G. Wells, 'The Remarkable Case of Davidson's Eyes', supplies what may be a more representative image – a laboratory worker after an accident, 'seeing what at the time we imagined was an altogether phantasmal world, and stone blind to the world around him'; living in Hampstead village, but simultaneously existing amidst the horrors of a bleak penguin island, which turned out to have an actual existence. The narrator is baffled.

> 'Explanation there is none forthcoming, except what Professor Wade has thrown out. But his explanation invokes the Fourth Dimension, and a dissertation on theoretical kinds of space. To talk of there being "a kink in space" seems mere nonsense to me; it may be because I am no mathematician.'

> H.G. Wells, *The Stolen Bacillus and Other Incidents* (1895), pp.184; 190.

In the first draft of *The Time Machine* (March–June 1894), Wells referred to the astronomer and mathematician Simon Newcomb, who had lectured on four-dimensional geometry to the New York Mathematical Society in 1893 (Philmus and Hughes, pp.49; 59), but it is arguable that scholarly effort to find an exact context for references to 'the Fourth Dimension' is subverted by an individual author's well-known freedom in inventing 'facts' that suit his narrative purpose and also by the habit of mind that can 'disdain the notion of Finality', even in the 'exact sciences'. To parody Samuel Johnson on the nature of dramatic illusion in 1765: surmise, if surmise be admitted, has no certain limitation.

2 Palaeontology, Geology, Zoology, Biology

A History of Extinctions

During the first decades of the nineteenth century, attention shifted from mineralogy, the study of inorganic matter, to palaeontology, the study of the fossils of extinct animals and plants found in the rocks. The great comparative anatomist G.F. de Cuvier, who would confidently infer the structure of an entire extinct creature from a single bone, is cited by Byron.

> The reader will perceive that the author has partly adopted in this poem the notion of Cuvier, that the world had been destroyed several times before the creation of man. This speculation, derived from the strata and the bones of enormous and unknown animals found in them, is not contrary to the Mosaic account, ...
>
> Lord Byron, *Cain: A Mystery* (1821), Prefatory Note.

Byron is being cautious, since the Bible was traditionally thought to have dated the Creation at 4004 BC and now a series of creations was being suggested. Cuvier argued that each fossil species was so exactly suited to its physical environment that it would become extinct if the surface of the earth changed in any radical way. His 1812 study of the fossils and strata of the Paris basin indicated to him that whole sets of fixed species had been successively replaced after catastrophes and floods, the last of which, some thought, might have been Noah's Flood. Forms like the Siberian mammoth, resembling modern species of elephant but not identical with them, are to be found in superficial deposits.

Cain   And those enormous creatures,

*   *   *

Resembling somewhat the wild inhabitants
Of the deep woods of earth, the hugest which
Roar nightly in the forest, but ten-fold
In magnitude and terror; taller than
The cherub-guarded walls of Eden, with
Eyes flashing like the fiery swords which fence them,
And tusks projecting like the trees stripp'd of
Their bark and branches – what were they?
Lucifer   That which
The Mammoth is in thy world; but these lie
By myriads underneath its surface.

Lord Byron, Cain: A Mystery (1821), II.ii.132-44,
pp.41-42.

Byron had a definite grasp of such phenomena as 'the occurrence of fossils in caves and fissure pitfalls' and the explanations offered by contemporary diluvial geology. The following passage is full of prophecies of a cataclysmal inundation to come:

Japhet   In a few days,
Perhaps even hours, ye will be changed, rent, hurled
Before the mass of waters; and yon cave,
Which seems to lead into a lower world,
Shall have its depths search'd by the sweeping wave,
And dolphins gambol in the lion's den!

*   *   *

Chorus of Spirits issuing from the cavern
We, we shall view the deep salt sources pour'd
Until one element shall do the work
   Of all in chaos; until they,
   The creatures proud of their poor clay,
Shall perish, and their bleached bones shall lurk

In caves, in dens, in clefts of mountains, where
The Deep shall follow to their latest lair;
    Where even the brutes, in their despair,
Shall cease to prey on man and on each other,
    And the striped tiger shall lie down to die
Beside the lamb, ...

Lord Byron, *Heaven and Earth: A Mystery* (1823),
I.iii.8-13; 170-80, pp.22; 30-31.

Byron's grandiose verse should be read beside William
Buckland's popular classic, *Reliquae Diluvianae; or,
Observations on the Organic Remains Contained in Caves,
Fissures, and Diluvial Gravel, and on Other Geological
Phenomena, Attesting the Action of an Universal Deluge.*

A deep hole nearly perpendicular, and bones quite
perfect, lodged in irregular heaps in the lowest pits, and
in cavities along the lateral enlargements of this hole,
and mixed with mud, pebbles, and fragments of
limestone, in precisely the same manner as I shall
hereafter show them to be lodged and mixed in the
caves and fissures of Germany and Gibraltar; and as
they would have been, supposing they were drifted to
their present place by the diluvian waters from some
lodgment which they had before obtained in the upper
regions of these extensive and connected cavities. That
they are of antediluvian origin is evident from the
presence of the extinct hyaena, tiger, and rhinoceros;
but there still remains a difficulty in ascertaining what
was the place from which they were so drifted; . . . .
The third hypothesis is that which I propose as most
probable, viz. that the animals had fallen during the
antediluvian period into the open fissures, and there
perishing, had remained undisturbed in the spot on
which they died, till drifted forwards by the diluvian
waters to their present place in the lowest vaultings with
which these fissures had communication . . . .

William Buckland, *Reliquae Diluvianae* (1823),
1834 edn, pp.76; 78.

The early nineteenth century became acutely aware that palaeontology was proving that there had been an immensely long series of extinct life-forms before human beings had even appeared on the earth. Also zoology showed, in the case of the dodo, that creatures living in comparatively recent times (the seventeenth century) could vanish from the world as a species – a commonplace now but a matter of controversy in the first decades of the century. N.A. Rupke tells us that Buckland's work gave rise to a number of literary responses, from comic verses on 'The Last British Hyaena', by P.B. Duncan,

> Thus did he growl aloud his last bequest –
> "My skull to William Buckland I bequeath."

＊　　＊　　＊

> Southward a flood from Yorkshire chanced to travel,
> And rolled the monster deep in Rugby gravel

to the sardonic metaphors of J.S. Mill on English law: 'Every struggle which ever rent the bosom of society is apparent in the disjointed condition of the part of the field of law which covers the spot; nay, the very traps and pitfalls which one contending party set for another are still standing, and the teeth not of hyaenas only but of foxes and all cunning animals are imprinted on the curious remains found in these antediluvian caves'. (Rupke, *The Great Chain of History*, pp.72-80.) But it would be hard to match the satiric verve with which Byron handled the whole business of catastrophes and relics of 'a former world' in *Don Juan*. He there imagines a future time,

> When this world shall be *former*, underground,
>   Thrown topsy-turvy, twisted, crisp'd, and curl'd,
> Baked, fried, or burnt, turn'd inside-out, or drown'd,
>   Like all the worlds before, which have been hurl'd
> First out of, and then back again to chaos,
> The superstratum which will overlay us.

So Cuvier says: – and then shall come again
    Unto the new creation, rising out
From our old crash, some mystic, ancient strain
    Of things destroy'd and left in airy doubt;
Like to the notions we now entertain
    Of Titans, giants, fellows of about
Some hundred feet in height, *not* to say *miles*,
And mammoths, and your wingèd crocodiles.

Think if then George the Fourth should be dug up,
    How the new worldlings of the then new East
Will wonder where such animals could sup!

Lord Byron, *Don Juan*, Canto 9 (1823),
stanzas 37-39, *Poetical Works*, ed. J.D. Jump, 1970,
pp.773-74.

Byron handles with ease the controversy between Neptunists, who thought that early rocks such as granite had solidified out of an original chaotic ocean, and Plutonists (or Vulcanists), who stressed the action of fire. He had a sure imaginative grasp of the remote past, though contemporary palaeontology was producing some exaggerated estimates of size. Buckland calculated that the megalosaur ('great lizard') had been some sixty or seventy feet long and the iguanadon ('teeth like an iguana's') was thought to have reached one hundred feet. More accurate estimates were made of other discoveries in the great decade 1814–1824, the aquatic reptiles ichthyosaur ('fish lizard')·and plesiosaur ('akin to the lizard'), but ideas of how they looked and behaved inevitably made them resemble the dragons of fable. This newly discovered world in time, earlier and far more terrible than the one of hyaenas and cave-bears mainly depicted in *Reliquae Diluvianae*, was completed by the discovery of the pterodactyl ('wing finger'). Buckland gives an animated description of them all in a learned article for the Geological Society.

With flocks of such-like creatures flying in the air, and shoals of no less monstrous Ichthyosauri and

Plesiosauri swarming in the ocean, and gigantic crocodiles and tortoises crawling on the shores of the primaeval lakes and rivers, – air, sea, and land must have been strangely tenanted in these early periods of our infant world.

Transactions of the Geological Society, 2nd Series, Vol. 3, 1835, p.222.

The monsters caught the public imagination, soon appeared in children's books and one even found its clumsy way into the first paragraph of *Bleak House*. We may suspect that Dickens intended more than incidental animation of local prose texture, however.

London. Michaelmas term lately over, and the Lord Chancellor sitting in Lincoln's Inn Hall. Implacable November weather. As much mud in the streets, as if the waters had but newly retired from the face of the earth, and it would not be wonderful to meet a Megalosaurus, forty feet long or so, waddling like an elephantine lizard up Holborn Hill. Smoke lowering down from chimney-pots, making a soft black drizzle, with flakes of soot in it as big as full-grown snow-flakes – gone into mourning, one might imagine, for the death of the sun. Dogs, undistinguishable in mire. Horses, scarcely better; splashed to their very blinkers.

Charles Dickens, *Bleak House* (1852–53).

The bizarre juxtaposition of a megalosaurus with London dogs and cab-horses is an effective stroke in yet another scheme of this complex work: England's legal and political institutions are vestiges of an obsolete creation, fit to be destroyed.

Byron and Dickens treat the long sequence of extinctions with a grim vitality that was not shared by all writers. Individuals perish; even great races like the dinosaurs (*OED*, 1841: 'terrible lizards') have perished. Contemplation could bring despair.

The wish, that of the living whole
   No life may fail beyond the grave,
   Derives it not from what we have
The likest God within the soul?

Are God and Nature then at strife
   That Nature lends such evil dreams?
   So careful of the type she seems,
So careless of the single life;

          *   *   *

'So careful of the type?' but no.
   From scarped cliff and quarried stone
   She cries, 'A thousand types are gone:
I care for nothing, all shall go.

'Thou makest thine appeal to me:
   I bring to life, I bring to death:
   The spirit does but mean the breath:
I know no more.' And he, shall he,

Man, her last work, who seem'd so fair,
   Such splendid purpose in his eyes,
   Who roll'd the psalm to wintry skies,
Who built him fanes of fruitless prayer,

Who trusted God was love indeed
   And love Creation's final law –
   Tho' Nature, red in tooth and claw
With ravine, shriek'd against his creed –

Who loved, who suffer'd countless ills,
   Who battled for the True, the Just,
   Be blown about the desert dust,
Or seal'd within the iron hills?

No more? A monster then, a dream,
   A discord. Dragons of the prime,
   That tare each other in their slime,
Were mellow music match'd with him.

> Lord Tennyson, *In Memoriam* (1850), Sections 55
> and 56, ed. S. Shatto and Marion Shaw, (Oxford, 1982),
> pp.79-80.

The interplay between the hostile, appalling landscape Tennyson found in geology and palaeontology and the more 'nurturing cosmos' often associated with astronomy ('To feel once more, in placid awe, / The strong imagination roll / A sphere of stars about my soul') is a major pattern of the whole poem. (Gliserman, *Victorian Studies*, Vol. 18, 1974–75, pp.445-54.)

Towards the end of the century, however, the swift processes of cultural erosion had effaced the earlier terrors.

> Who he was who first, without ever having gone out to the rude chase, told the wondering cave-men at sunset how he had dragged the Megatherium from the purple darkness of its jasper cave, or slain the Mammoth in single combat and brought back its gilded tusks, we cannot tell, and not one of our modern anthropologists, with all their much-boasted science, has had the ordinary courage to tell us. Whatever was his name or race, he was certainly the true founder of social intercourse. For the aim of the liar is simply to charm, to delight, to give pleasure. He is the very basis of civilised society, and without him a dinner party, even at the mansions of the great, is as dull as a lecture at the Royal Society or a debate at the Incorporated Authors.

> Oscar Wilde, 'The Decay of Lying', *The Nineteenth Century*, Vol. 25, 1889, pp.45-46.

Progressive Development

Biological studies begin with the crowded, fertile life of this planet as it divides, buds, sprouts and germinates in time – time geologically extended, zoologically multiplied and apparently unlimited in its variations. Even in the eighteenth century, the naturalist Carl Linnaeus had listed no less than 14 000 species, of which about 5600 were animals, which caused him to give up belief in the historical reality of Noah's Ark altogether. Later, in a famous summary article called 'The Development Hypothesis' Herbert Spencer estimated the number of existing and extinct species combined at some ten millions (*The Leader*, 20 March 1852). The various kinds of evolutionary theory that became so important in the central decades of the nineteenth century fired the imagination. Biological change is not simple and uniform, despite the early attempts to make it so. The work of Darwin and Wallace showed it to thrive on mutation, divergence and transformation. In many respects it proved to be more compatible with the typical richness and profusion of high Victorian literature, art and architecture, which makes R.L. Stevenson's claim that 'a proposition of geometry is a fair and luminous parallel for a work of art', because both 'are reasonable, both untrue to the crude fact, both inhere in nature, neither represents it' (*Longman's Magazine*, Vol. 5, 1885, p.143) seems a late and theoretical counter-reaction belonging to the context of the exact sciences. The biological sciences are usually closer in literary practice, though often disconcertingly so.

The notion that humans are related to the higher animals is very old. The classical figure of the satyr, goat-like and lustful, was taken by Spenser and made into a moral reproach to civilised man. Spenser's Sir Satyrane in Book 1 of the *Faerie Queene* is, ironically, one of nature's gentlemen. Peacock brings this figure scientifically more up-to-date by introducing a speechless but otherwise gravely civilised baronet, Sir Oran Haut-Ton, who was supposed to have been caught as a young orang-utan in Angolan forests. (John C. Greene has described the confusion between the orang-utan of East Asia and the chimpanzee of Africa in *The Death of Adam* (1959), pp.187-94.)

> Some presumptuous naturalists have refused his species the honours of humanity; but the most enlightened and illustrious philosophers agree in

considering him in his true light as the natural and original man. One French philosopher, indeed, has been guilty of an inaccuracy, in considering him as a degenerated man: degenerated he cannot be; as his prodigious physical strength, his uninterrupted health, and his amiable simplicity of manners demonstrate.

T.L. Peacock, *Melincourt* (1817), Chapter 6, Vol. 1, pp.67-70.

Peacock's flights of comic fancy are ballasted by an apparatus of learned footnotes, which cite late eighteenth-century authorities like James Burnet, Lord Monboddo. Monboddo was thought to be rather cranky by his contemporaries, but his classification of human beings with the orang-utans and his assertion that 'Man is in this life in a state of progression, from the mere Animal to the intellectual Creature, of greater or less perfection' (Greene, *The Death of Adam* pp.212-13) came to look less and less foolish in the next century. To Peacock in 1817, however, Monboddo provided a means of attacking so-called civilised society with a splendidly droll character.

Mr. Oran had long before shown a taste for music, and, with some little instruction from a marine officer in the Tornado, had become a proficient on the flute and French horn. He could never be brought to understand the notes; but from hearing any simple tune played or sung two or three times, he never failed to perform it with great exactness and brilliance of execution. I shall merely observe, *en passant*, that music appears, from this and several similar circumstances, to be more natural to man than speech. The old Captain was fond of his bottle of wine after dinner, and his glass of grog at night. Mr. Oran was easily brought to sympathize in this taste; and they have many times sat up together half the night over a flowing bowl, the old Captain singing Rule Britannia, True Courage, or Tom Tough, and Sir Oran accompanying him on the French horn.

Ibid., pp.75-77.

Biological development as it came to be conceived in the nineteenth century required a vast time scale. Besides the palaeontological theories we have seen in Buckland, a major work of scholarship, Charles Lyell's *Principles of Geology* (3 vols, 1830–33), cautiously rejected the claim that Noah's Flood – or even a series of floods and catastrophes – could account for the complicated geological facts of the earth's crust. Instead Lyell emphasised the protracted and continuous effects of 'Causes Now in Operation': not only earthquakes and volcanoes but alluvial deposits, erosion and the like. Whewell dubbed this 'uniformitarianism' and its opposite 'catastrophism'. Lyell's rejection of catastrophism also led him to disagree with Cuvier's belief that successive faunas appearing after each cataclysm were animals of a higher type than before. This infinitely seductive idea was very definitely present in a popular book published anonymously in 1844, *Vestiges of the Natural History of Creation* by Robert Chambers, together with the suggestion that species themselves were mutable.

Chambers' amateur effort 'to connect the natural sciences into a history of creation' (p.388) is scientifically inaccurate in much of its detail, sometimes ludicrously so, but it would be hard to overestimate the cultural importance of his timely and effectively written synthesis. He brought together geology and biology in particular, to argue for organic development, the origin of species (including human kind) by natural descent. Catastrophism had often been linked with mysterious causes, frequent 'special creations' by divine intervention and the almost complete stability of species whilst they existed on the earth. Chambers asserted that God had first created all but then argued that species had both originated and been transformed by natural processes. After the planets had been thrown off from a whirling 'nebulous star', the earth went through various stages of progressive development that were not yet completed. The brightest of futures seemed to beckon.

> We must now call to mind that the geographical distribution of plants and animals was very different in the geological ages from what it is now. Down to a time not long antecedent to man, the same vegetation

overspread every clime, and a similar uniformity marked the zoology. This is conceived by M.[A.] Brogniart, with great plausibility, to have been the result of a uniformity of climate, produced by the as yet unexhausted effect of the internal heat of the earth upon its surface; . . . . It may have been that the multitudes of locally peculiar species only came into being after the uniform climate had passed away. It may have only been when a varied climate arose, that the originally few species branched off into the present extensive variety. . . .

Man, then, considered zoologically, and without regard to the distinct character assigned to him by theology, simply takes his place as the type of all types of the animal kingdom, the true and unmistakable head of animated nature upon this earth. . . .

Is our race but the initial of the grand crowning type? Are there yet to be species superior to us in organization, purer in feeling, more powerful in device and act, and who shall take a rule over us! There is in this nothing improbable on other grounds. The present race, rude and impulsive as it is, is perhaps the best adapted to the present state of things in the world; but the external world goes through slow and gradual changes, which may leave it in time a much serener field of existence. There may then be occasion for a nobler type of humanity, which shall complete the zoological circle on this planet, and realize some of the dreams of the purest spirits of the present race.

Robert Chambers, *Vestiges of the Natural History of Creation* (1844), pp.261-62; 272-73; 276.

Tennyson may not have read *Vestiges* (or reviews of it) until a relatively late stage in the composition of the many lyrics of *In Memoriam* but there are obvious similarities in some of the more optimistic of them.

They say
The solid earth whereon we tread

In tracts of fluent heat began,
   And grew to seeming-random forms,
   The seeming prey of cyclic storms,
Till at the last arose the man;

Who throve and branch'd from clime to clime,
   The herald of a higher race,
   And of himself in higher place,
If so he type this work of time

Within himself, from more to more;
   Or, crown'd with attributes of woe
   Like glories, move his course, and show
That life is not as idle ore,

But iron dug from central gloom,
   And heated hot with burning fears,
   And dipt in baths of hissing tears,
And batter'd with the shocks of doom

To shape and use. Arise and fly
   The reeling Faun, the sensual feast;
   Move upward, working out the beast,
And let the ape and tiger die.

> Lord Tennyson, *In Memoriam* (1850), Section 118,
> eds Shatto and Shaw, p.133.

Peacock and Monboddo were rather more respectful to the organic beings with whom we are 'bound together in development, and in a system of both affinites and analogies' (R. Chambers, *Vestiges*, p.251).

The future of humanity, however, was a leading theme in European culture. In his preface to *The Excursion* (1814) Wordsworth had written some lines which could be regarded as prophetic of this strain of biological optimism.

       . . . my voice proclaims
How exquisitely the individual Mind
(And the progressive powers perhaps no less
Of the whole species) to the external World
Is fitted.

John Herschel's immensely influential *A Preliminary Discourse on the Study of Natural Philosophy* (1831) is based on a central conviction that science shows us 'our strength and innate dignity' as a race in that it calls upon faculties and powers 'which form, as it were, a link between ourselves and the best and noblest benefactors of our species, with whom we hold communion in thoughts and participate in discoveries which have raised them above their fellow-mortals, and brought them nearer their Creator' (1832 edn, pp.16-17). The most famous Victorian expression of such aspirations is found in the Epilogue of *In Memoriam*, when Tennyson finally proclaims his dead friend Hallam 'a closer link / Betwixt us and the crowning race'

> Of those that, eye to eye, shall look
>   On knowledge; under whose command
>   Is Earth and Earth's, and in their hand
> Is Nature like an open book;
>
> No longer half-akin to brute,
>   For all we thought and loved and did,
>   And hoped, and suffer'd, is but seed
> Of what in them is flower and fruit;
>
> Whereof the man, that with me trod
>   This planet, was a noble type
>   Appearing ere the times were ripe,
> That friend of mine who lives in God,
>
> That God, which ever lives and loves,
>   One God, one law, one element,
>   And one far-off divine event,
> To which the whole creation moves.

> Lord Tennyson, *In Memoriam* (1850), Epilogue,
> ll.127-44.

Palaeontology and geology might bring despair, zoology arouse satirical comparisons but Chambers' developmental biology could evidently be retained within a providential frame of reference and contribute powerfully to the anthropocentric, human-centred vision of early nineteenth-century culture. The cost was the distancing of God from creation and the removal of the origin of the universe to the remotest past.

> We have seen powerful evidence, that the construction of this globe and its associates, and inferentially that of all the other globes of space, was the result, not of any immediate or personal exertion on the part of the Deity, but of natural laws which are expressions of his will. What is to hinder our supposing that the organic creation is also a result of natural laws, which are in like manner an expression of his will?
>
> Robert Chambers, *Vestiges of the Natural History of Creation* (1844), pp.153-54.

Emotionally many regretted the exchange of a present, caring God for 'natural laws', unless they could, as Tennyson did, replace Him with a caring cosmos and keep their gaze firmly fixed on that 'one far-off divine event'. Scientifically, however, the ways in which organic change was actually brought about in Chambers' scheme seemed implausible – through foetal monstrosities, for example (pp.218-19).

In his introduction to a modern reprint of *Vestiges* Gavin de Beer judges that Chambers had successfully recognised 'the parallelism between stages of embryonic development, categories of classification, and series of fossils' (p.28). The human embryo 'gradually passes through conditions generally resembling a fish, a reptile, a bird, and the lower mammalia', Chambers wrote; 'the resemblance is not to the adult fish or the adult reptile, but to the fish and reptile at a certain point in their foetal progress' (Chambers, *Vestiges*, pp.199; 212). In his second formulation Chambers correctly expressed K.E. von Baer's belief that the resemblances were between embryos only but many authors in the nineteenth century interpreted the gill slits observable in human embryos as those of adult fishy ancestors. The first formulation from Chambers seems to offer a rapid, condensed 'recapitulation' in the womb of the complete evolution of the human species. It also indicates opportunities for deliberate satire. Disraeli had two of his characters discuss a book called 'The Revelations of Chaos' – undoubtedly *Vestiges of Creation* – which 'explains everything, and is written in a very agreeable style'.

> 'But what is most interesting, is the way in which man has been developed. You know, all is development. The principle is perpetually going on. First, there was nothing, then there was something; then – I forget the next – I think there were shells, then fishes; then we came – let me see – did we come next? Never mind that; we came at last. And the next change there will be something very superior to us – something with wings. Ah! that's it: we were fishes, and I believe we shall be crows. But you must read it.'
> 'I do not believe I ever was a fish,' said Tancred.

> Benjamin Disraeli, *Tancred* (1847), Chapter 9,
> Vol. 1, pp.224-46.

S.J. Gould's learned book demonstrates the 'lamentable confusion' that afflicted von Baer's idea of the relationship between ontogeny (individual life history) and phylogeny (species development) but such confusions can be regarded as the chaotic primaeval ocean in which new literary life appears and flourishes. We can see Tennyson using both catastrophism and uniformitarianism, as well as the organic development of Chambers and that of Lamarck, to which the former did not subscribe. Misunderstandings, contradictions and jostling confusions have creative value.

Lamarckian Evolution

Chambers made a delightfully Edward Lear-like suggestion that a goose might accidentally produce an offspring with the body of a rat, resembling a duck-billed platypus, which in its turn might supply the appropriate mouth and feet, thus producing a true rat and completing 'at two stages the passage from the aves to the mammalia' (Chambers, *Vestiges*, p.219)!

There was, however, a more plausible theory of how one species of plants or animals could change bodily into another, of evolution in the sense of transformation of earlier forms (*OED*, 1832), proposed by J.B. de Lamarck in 1809. Briefly, environmental changes bring about changes in needs (*besoins*) and therefore in behaviour. In time new habits lead to development or atrophy of organs, which are transmitted in these modified forms to progeny. In the second volume of his *Principles*, where *evolution* was first used in its modern sense, Charles Lyell gave a somewhat sceptical summary of Lamarck's ideas, which remained almost unchanged through successive revisions and was probably the main channel of information about them in Britain.

> Every considerable alteration in the local circumstances in which each race of animals exists, causes a change in their wants, and these new wants excite them to new actions and habits. These actions require the more frequent employment of some parts before but slightly exercised, and then greater development follows as a consequence of their more frequent use. Other organs no longer in use are impoverished and diminished in size, nay, are sometimes entirely annihilated, while in their place new parts are insensibly produced for the discharge of new functions.
>
> ... when the possibility of the indefinite modification of individuals descending from common parents was once assumed, as also the geological generalization [*later*, inference] respecting the progressive development of organic life, it was natural that ... the most simple and imperfect forms and faculties should be conceived to have been the originals whence all others were developed.
>
> Charles Lyell, *Principles*, Vol. 2, 1832, Chapter 1: 'Lamarck on the Transmutation of Species', pp.7-8; 12.

Lyell calmly omits 'the mode whereby, after a countless succession of generations, a small gelatinous body is transformed into an oak or an ape', and passes to 'the last grand step in the progressive scheme', to describe how the cleverest race of orang-utans, the Angolan, gradually lost the habit of climbing trees and began to walk upright. Driven by 'the natural *tendency to perfection*' – an important assumption, as Lyell's italics show – they gradually became dominant, felt the necessity of communicating new ideas in new circumstances and developed the faculty of speech, whilst inferior creatures were driven into conditions where the development of their faculties was actually retarded. It is a clear and judicious account, but remains as inert 'background to literature'.

But dilute 'a countless succession' to a few generations; stress the efforts and desires of the organisms concerned (*besoins* can mean 'wants' as well as 'needs'), and this ever-popular theory becomes available for socio-political purposes. Neo-Lamarckian ideas can be used to provide an environmental explanation of human ills, together with a stimulus to intelligent self-development and positive alteration of conditions. An article by William Thompson entitled 'Physical argument for the *equal* cultivation of all the useful faculties or capabilities, mental or physical, of men and women' (1826) explicitly acknowledges Lamarck's thesis that individuals gain or lose faculties 'by the influence of the circumstances to which their race has been for a long time exposed', and then rather hopefully applies it to human society along with an idea from a new science, *phrenology* (*OED*, 1815).

> What stupendous intellectual and moral effects may we not expect to be produced in the human species, when the physical and mental powers of both the parents shall be equally cultivated, amongst whom even now, education operating on improved susceptibilities can effect such wonders as we every day see it to produce? particularly when we take into account the facts lately ascertained and placed beyond doubt by the philosophical enquirers into the mode of operating and developments of the brain, that changes produced by education inducing new social and intellectual qualities, produce analogous changes in the structure of the brain

as indicated by changes of form in its external bony covering, the cranium?

Quoted by John Killham in *Tennyson and 'The Princess': Reflections of an Age* (1958), pp.271-72.

The same mixture of Neo-Lamarckian, phrenological and feminist ideas can be found in *The Princess: A Medley* when Tennyson deals with the topical issue of a college for women. Just as geology and palaeontology were often considered in a religious light, not a purely scientific one, so evolutionary biology attracted socio-political and educational attention from writers of the time.

> 'Deep, indeed,
> Their debt of thanks to her who first had dared
> To leap the rotten pales of prejudice,
> Disyoke their necks from custom, and assert
> None lordlier than themselves but that which made
> Woman and man. She had founded; they must build.
> Here might they learn whatever men were taught:
> Let them not fear: some said their heads were less:
> Some men's were small; not they the least of men;
> For often fineness compensated size:
> Besides the brain was like the hand, and grew
> With using; thence the man's, if more was more;
> He took advantage of his strength to be
> First in the field: some ages had been lost;'

Lord Tennyson, *The Princess: A Medley* (1847), ed. C. Ricks (1969), Part 2, ll.124-37.

If brains and hands have thus grown in use, we are in the thought-world of Lamarck, where snakes grow longer as they strive to meet challenges and lose the legs they fail to use in holes and crevices. One imagines that Lamarck himself must have been driven by 'satiable curtiosity, like the elephant's child in Kipling's *Just So Stories*!

A somewhat different mixture can be found in Charles Kingsley's *Alton Locke* (1850). This is a typical 'Condition of England' novel, rooted in urban squalor and class conflict, but it contains an evolutionary myth of loss and degeneration as well as recovery. Its hero is made to relive the history of life on earth in a chapter-long dream, a narrative device that allows Kingsley's liberated imagination to incorporate fantastic sequences and poetically sensuous prose in what is basically a realistic novel.

> And I was at the lowest point of created life: a madrepore [coral] rooted to the rock, fathoms below the tide-mark; and, worst of all, my individuality was gone. I was not one thing, but many things – a crowd of innumerable polypi; . . . .
> And Eleanor said, 'He who falls from the golden ladder must climb through ages to its top. He who tears himself in pieces by his lusts, ages only can make him one again. The madrepore shall become a shell, and the shell a fish, and the fish a bird, and the bird a beast; and then he shall become a man again, and see the glory of the latter days.'

> Charles Kingsley, *Alton Locke* (1850), Chapter 36, Vol. 2, pp.214-15; ed. E.A. Cripps, (Oxford, 1983), pp.336-37.

Christian morality and phraseology mingle curiously with the sea life which assumed such importance in evolutionary biology. Erasmus Darwin's motto had been 'Omnia ex Conchis' ('All from Oysters'), and Lamarck believed that life had begun with the simplest and least perfect of forms in the primaeval ocean. Kingsley's Chapter 36 also illustrates how Neo-Lamarckian cravings ('And I felt stirring in me germs of a new and higher consciousness – yearnings of love towards the mother ape, who fed me and carried me from tree to tree') interact with Socialist instincts on the upward stages of the ascent ('So we were all equal – for none took more than he needed; and we were all free, because we loved to obey the king by whom the spirit spoke; and we were all brothers, because we had one work, and one hope, and one All-Father'). This chapter, with its reference to 'some ideal of the great Arian tribe, containing in herself all future types of European women' trenches on anthropological concerns to be discussed later, as does its dream-structure. It defies simple interpretation, though as a whole one might see it as a scientific variant of an ancient Biblical myth: 'You went forth with the world a wilderness before you – you shall return when it is a garden behind you. You went forth selfish savages – you shall return as the brothers of the Son of God' (*Alton Locke*, Vol. 2, p.236) – another Fortunate Fall, but far back into a past ruled only by small gelatinous bodies and oysters.

The extent of academic opposition to Lamarckian ideas may be judged from Whewell's review of Lyell in the *Quarterly Review* for 1832, 'intended for general readers'. He refused to accept any analogy between the slow changes postulated by uniformitarian geology and organic 'transmutation' of species: such theories were, in his terms, visionary, unauthorised, loose and headlong, in the highest degree hypothetical, and indeed extravagantly gratuitous, untenable, strange, sweeping, fantastic, wild, unphilosophical and utterly futile! Of course, he used arguments. Domestic plants and animals are modified, but within limits, not indefinitely. Nor do such modified species endure. Released into the wild, 'the refined flavour and polished exterior of the products of the orchard are assailed by a democratic aggression of thorns and brambles; and, in the struggle, they either perish, or preserve their place only by becoming as coarse and rude as their neighbours' (*Quarterly Review*, Vol. 47, 1832, p.133). This joke, in the year of the First Reform Act of Parliament, reminds us again of socio-political implications. There are religious implications, too. Whewell suggests that 'so far as we can trace the history of the new families and species which have inhabited the earth, they have made their appearance exactly *as if* they have been placed there, each by an express act of the Creator' (p.117), and he makes fun of a man who attempted a compromise between Biblical and evolutionary history by claiming that in previous epochs our ancestors had maintained 'a sort of perpetual dictatorship in the creation', but were physically adapted to a different environment, such as a poisonous atmosphere of carbonic acid. It was also suggested that the longevity of Biblical patriarchs 'indicates an order of things more like what now takes place among reptiles and fishes'. This was too much. Whewell sarcastically looked forward to discovering how far the patriarchs resembled crocodiles and sharks when their fossil remains turned up; 'we shall receive with no small delight the restoration of the *Patriarchosauros*, which Mr [W.D.] Conybeare, in his double capacity of divine and saurologist, will no doubt feel himself bound to undertake' (pp.116-17). This bizarre evocation underlines the 'cultural interchange' of ideas and fictions which can be found whenever academic neutrality is abandoned and the fancy given free rein. Whewell's imaginative derision reminds us more of Byron or Peacock than any strictly scientific author. Nor is his outlook untypical, the classic instance being Philip Gosse's perfectly serious suggestion that Adam, though not born of woman, must have had an omphalos or navel. He assumed a circle of organic creation (chicken to egg to chicken, etc) which, if God initiated it at any point, would naturally contain signs of the past all descendants were about to possess (Edmund Gosse, *Father and Son: A Study of Two Temperaments* (1907), ed. J. Hepburn, (1974), pp.61; 183). We realise that in the middle of the nineteenth century the conflict of scientific ideas about evolution, the piecemeal discovery of relevant evidence and the complex bearing of the whole on traditional ways of understanding life had together come to a public crisis.

Evolution by Natural Selection

The second main theory of biological evolution was devised by Alfred Wallace and Charles Darwin. Darwin's 1831–36 voyage around South America as naturalist on the *Beagle*, with Lyell's *Principles of Geology* and *The Poetical Works of John Milton* for reading matter, convinced him that the physical world had been and still was subject to continuous change through the action of natural forces. How then could species of plants and animals in such changeable conditions have remained fixed since the time of their creation? In his autobiography he tells us that he decided to collect as many facts as possible about variation. He knew that deliberate breeding programmes were successful in altering plant and animal types but it was a chance reading of 'Malthus on Population' that helped him realise how *natural* selection worked. Plants and animals could not increase their own means of subsistence as their populations increased. In the ensuing struggle for existence 'favourable variations would tend to be preserved and unfavourable ones destroyed. The result of this would be the formation of new species', Darwin concluded (*Autobiographies*, ed. de Beer, pp.70-71). Biology, interacting with geology and demography, was now poised to become the leading science of the age. We should not, however, forget how well Darwin knew his Milton; *Comus* especially contains a very un-Malthusian view of the value of natural fertility, which in practice must multiply the number of possibly favourable variations.

In 1842 Darwin wrote in pencil an abstract of his theory of evolution by means of natural selection, but then immersed himself for years in a study of barnacles, fossil and living, found in his own collections and in the British Museum, borrowed from friends and obtained from all over the globe. (He always thought that he must be the original of the Professor Long who had written two huge volumes on limpets in Bulwer's novel *What Will He Do With It?*, 1858.) Darwin's leisurely preparations were interrupted in 1858 by a beautifully clear essay on his central idea of 'natural selection' by the naturalist Alfred Wallace, then in the Malay Archipelago.

> The hypothesis of Lamarck – that progressive changes in species have been produced by the attempts of animals to increase the development of their own organs, and thus modify their structure and habits – has been repeatedly and easily refuted by all writers on the subject of varieties and species, and it seems to have been considered that when this was done the whole question has been finally settled; but the view here developed renders such an hypothesis quite unnecessary, by showing that similar results must be produced by the action of principles constantly at work in nature. The powerful retractile talons of the falcon – and the cat-tribes have not been produced or increased by the volition of these animals; but among the different varieties which occurred in the earliest and less highly organized forms of these groups, *those always*

survived longest which had the greatest facilities for seizing their prey. . . . animals, especially insects, so closely resembling the soil or the leaves or the trunks on which they habitually reside, are explained on the same principle; for though in the course of ages varieties of many tints have occurred, *yet those races having colours best adapted to concealment from their enemies would inevitably survive the longest.*

'On the Tendency of Varieties to Depart
Indefinitely from the Original Type', *Journal of* . . .
the Linnean Society, Vol. 3, 1859.

A combined announcement was made on their behalf by colleagues to the Linnean Society of London on 1 July 1858. Darwin's much longer book, *On the Origin of Species by Means of Natural Selection, or the Preservation of Favoured Races in the Struggle for Life*, was published in the following year.

It is, Darwin insisted in Chapter 4, a 'principle of preservation', 'called, for the sake of brevity, Natural Selection' (p.127). Those organisms survive that are fit to survive in a particular time and place. No intention or purpose is invoked. Orthodox morality is irrelevant. Change and transformation are in the long term inescapable, since variations occurring by chance enter an utterly conditional existence. They either are, or are not, advantageous; and 'from the strong principle of inheritance', which Darwin believed in as much as Lamarck, useful variations will probably be transmitted to offspring. The *Origin* is cautiously reticent on the subject of human beings but Darwin added a sentence so that no one could accuse him of concealing his belief that mankind must come under the same law: 'Light will be thrown on the origin of man and his history' (*Autobiographies*, p.78). If what Darwin called 'a severe struggle for life' was not so obvious in Victorian Britain as it might be in more savage societies, he nevertheless provided a model of special value for prose fiction when he emphasised 'the infinite complexity of the relations of all organic beings to each other and to their conditions of existence, causing an infinite diversity in structure, constitution, and habits' (*Origin of Species*, p.127). It was an ever-changing model, for which his image was a great tree.

> At each period of growth all the growing twigs have tried to branch out on all sides, and to overtop and kill the surrounding twigs and branches, in the same manner as species and groups of species have tried to overmaster other species in the great battle for life. . . . Of the many twigs which flourished when the tree was a mere bush, only two or three, now grown into great branches, yet survive and bear all the other branches; so with the species which lived during long-past geological periods, very few now have living and modified descendants.
>
> Charles Darwin, *Origin of Species* (1859), p.129.

British culture in mid-century was already suffused with ideas of extinction, catastrophe and progressive development, as we have seen (pp.58-78 above). In a poem begun in 1852 Tennyson spoke of 'this changing world of changeless law' ('De Profundis', 1.6). With the *Origin of Species* in 1859 began a new phase of biological thought. Darwin wrote of 'law', but the changing world it predicted seemed far more uncontrollable and random. The web of interrelationships was 'an entangled bank' which made the magnetic system of Faradayan science seem stable in comparison. Hopkins could accept a world of flux, and even human impermanence ('Man, how fast his firedint,/his mark on mind is gone!'), because in this 'Heraclitean Fire' he had faith in the 'comfort of the Resurrection'. But such comfort came from outside the Darwinian scheme.

> When I look forth at dawning, pool,
> Field, flock, and lonely tree,
> All seem to gaze at me
> Like chastened children sitting silent in a school.

*   *   *

'Has some Vast Imbecility,
    Mighty to build and blend,
    But impotent to tend,
Framed us in jest, and left us now to hazardry?'

> Thomas Hardy, 'Nature's Questioning', stanzas
> 1;4.

There is no grandeur, beauty or wonder in this view of life. Darwin himself tells us in his autobiography that he had gradually lost orthodox religious faith: 'There seems to be no more design in the variability of organic beings and in the action of natural selection, than in the course which the wind blows' (*Autobiographies*, p.51). A spiritual east wind is blowing the cloud of mind into an unknowable future. There is no 'one far-off divine event / To which the whole creation moves', nor Browning's 'tendency to God' (*Paracelsus*, (1835), Part 5). Browning's dramatic monologue 'Caliban upon Setebos; or, Natural Theology in the Island' of 1864 draws the logical consequences of this view of life for many at the time, if not Darwin. He shows Shakespeare's monster Caliban defining his god Setebos as a being like himself – malicious, arbitrary, 'Giving just respite lest we die through pain, / Saving last pain for worst, – with which, an end' (ll.254-55).

Evolution and Literature

The *Origin of Species* gave Charles Kingsley the courage to release evolution from 'Dream Land', the title of Chapter 36 in *Alton Locke*. Very rapidly he wrote a story for children about a little chimney sweep who drowned but became a water baby with gills in an earlier phase of development. *The Water Babies* (1862–63) is a modern fairy tale, full of the wonders of natural metamorphosis and transformation, but it is also a work of fantasy which fastens on 'problems *within* Darwinian ideas or on problems *revealed by* evolutionary theory in relation to older world orders' (Gillian Beer, p.123). What might seem pure nonsense can be scientifically interpreted. 'If you have a hippopotamus major in your brain, you are no ape' (Chapter 4) punningly plays on Richard Owen's 'proof' that human beings were anatomically distinguished from other primates by having a 'hippocampus minor', a structure in the brain shaped like a sea horse in cross section – a fantastic parallel in itself. Huxley had demolished Owen's claim in 1858. One of the more unfortunate errors in *Vestiges of Creation* (1844) had been the idea that mites could be generated by electricity: 'Mr. Weekes observed one of the insects in the very act of emerging, immediately after which, it ascended to the surface of the fluid, and sought concealment in an obscure corner of the apparatus' (pp.186-87).

> So they were forced at last to let the poor professor ease his mind by writing a great book, exactly contrary to all his old opinions, in which he proved that the moon was made of green cheese, and that all the mites in it (which you may see sometimes quite plain through a telescope, if you will only keep the lens dirty enough, as Mr. Weekes kept his voltaic battery) are nothing in the world but little babies, who are hatching and swarming up there in millions, ready for the doctors to bring them in band-boxes at night, when children want a new little brother or sister.

Charles Kingsley, *The Water Babies*, Chapter 4,
Macmillan's Magazine, Vol. 7 (1862–63), pp.12-13.

The humour, however, conceals a sharp edge. It is comical enough that poor experiments should produce false results and that myopic old professors should make foolish assertions, but the thought of human babies hatching and swarming in millions, like mites, is a view of hyperfertility which can only appal if it is considered outside the bounds of an acknowledged fantasy. As Gillian Beer comments, 'In any transferred reading of evolutionary theory in human terms individualism is set under a new and almost intolerable tension by Darwin's emphasis on variability' (*Darwin's Plots*, p.127). Vast numbers are 'good', because they multiply the occurrence of potentially valuable mutations. They also ensure immense waste, bring death into this world and much of our woe. When little Tom, the sweep turned water baby, is picked up to be petted by Mrs Doasyouwouldbedoneby, she has to throw away 'great armfuls of babies – nine hundred under one arm, and thirteen hundred under the other.' Only in a myth do they 'not even take their thumbs out of their mouths, but come paddling and wriggling back to her like so many tadpoles . . . .' (Chapter 5).

In Chapter 3 'the great fairy Science' announces that 'your soul makes your body, just as a snail makes his shell'. It seems to give a Neo-Lamarckian turn to Coleridge's lines on the body as the 'Soul's self-symbol / its image of itself'. In more Darwinian terms, Kingsley the modern clergyman thought that scientists had 'got rid of an interfering God – a master magician, as I call it', so that now 'they have to choose between the absolute empire of accident, and a living, immanent, ever-working God' (To F.D. Maurice, [1863], *Letters*, ed. F. Kingsley, Vol. 2, p.171). The latter is not unlike Darwin's optimistic view of natural selection 'insensibly working . . . at the improvement of each organic being' (*Origin of Species*, Chapter 4). In *The Water Babies* natural selection becomes Mother Carey and her children, 'whom she makes out of the sea-water all day long'.

> He expected, of course, – like some grown people, who ought to know better – to find her snipping, piecing, fitting, stitching, cobbling, basting, filing, planing, hammering, turning, polishing, moulding, measuring, chiselling, clipping, and so forth, as men do when they go to work to make anything.
>
> But, instead of that, she sat quite still, with her chin upon her hand, looking down into the sea with two great grand blue eyes, as blue as the sea itself. . . .
>
> 'I heard, ma'am, that you were always making new beasts out of old.'
>
> 'So people fancy. But I am not going to trouble myself to make things, my little dear. I sit here and make them make themselves.'
>
> Charles Kingsley, *The Water Babies*, Chapter 7, *Macmillan's Magazine*, Vol. 7 (1862–63), pp.324-25.

Here Kingsley is emphasising the random aspect of Darwinian theory; favourable variations appear and are naturally selected. This modified creativity, however, is counterbalanced by darker fantasies elsewhere in the book. He writes of extinction, of the wingless Gairfowls: 'But men shot us so, and knocked us on the head, and took our eggs . . . .' (Chapter 7). In *Alice in Wonderland* (1865) Lewis Carroll somewhat gloomily chose the dodo to represent his childless, stammering self (Do-Do-Dodgson). Degeneration is presided over by 'a very tremendous lady' in *The Water Babies*, Mrs Bedonebyasyoudid, 'as old as Eternity, and yet as young as Time' (in Tennyson's 'changing world of changeless law'): 'If I can turn beasts into men, I can, by the same laws of circumstance, and selection, and competition, turn men into beasts'. This she illustrates, in a partly Lamarckian manner, by showing in a book of colour photographs – before such had been invented – the history of the lazy Doasyoulikes reverting to apes till the last one was shot, 'roaring and thumping his breast' and trying to say the old anti-slavery motto of an earlier period in the nineteenth century, 'Am I not a man and a brother?' (Chapter 6). Meredith discovered equally strenuous lessons in evolution.

> Behold the life at ease; it drifts.
> The sharpened life commands its course.
> She [Nature] winnows, winnows roughly; sifts,
> To dip her chosen in her source:
> Contestation is the vital force,
> Whence pluck they brain, her prize of gifts,
> Sky of the senses! On which height,
> Not disconnected, yet released,
> They see how spirit comes to light,
> Through conquest of the inner beast, ...
>
> George Meredith, 'Hard Weather', ll.71-80,
> in *A Reading of Earth* (1888).

Hence arises what is known as 'social Darwinism', the idea that the struggle for existence amongst humans would lead to social progress; individual suffering must be endured for the general good.

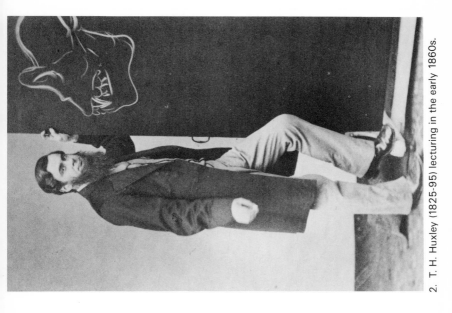

2. T. H. Huxley (1825-95) lecturing in the early 1860s.

1. Humphrey Davy (1778-1829) in 1804.

3. Alfred Tennyson (1809-92) in c.1840 by S. Laurence.

4. Charles Robert Darwin (1809-82), after the portrait by Maguire

5. Faraday lecturing at the Royal Institution before the Prince Consort and the Prince of Wales.

6. How the elephant got its trunk as featured in the *Just So Stories*, 1902, by Rudyard Kipling.

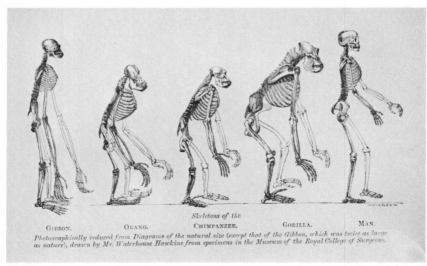

7. The frontispiece to T. H. Huxley's *Evidence as to Man's Place in Nature* (1863) which shows five skeletons progressing from a gibbon to a man.

Evolution and Major Novelists

George Eliot's *Middlemarch* (1871–72) contains frequent allusions to the exact sciences. Lydgate praises the scientific imagination for revealing 'subtle actions inaccessible by any sort of lens, but tracked in that outer darkness through long pathways of necessary sequence by the inward light which is the last refinement of Energy, capable of bathing even the etherial atoms in its ideally illuminated space' (Chapter 16). We might remember here that the planet Neptune had been discovered in 1846 by telescopic observation of a place in the heavens computed by a French theoretical astronomer and the young mathematician J.C. Adams, who had been inspired by two sentences in the sixth edition of Mary Somerville's *Connexion* suggesting that 'a body placed for ever beyond the sphere of vision' might be causing the failure of Uranus to follow its predicted orbit (*Personal Recollections of Mary Somerville* (1873), p.290). George Eliot also alludes to Kelvin's vortex atoms in the ether, which are based on Helmholtz's notion of endlessly whirling motion in a perfect fluid, but, as Maxwell wrote, 'the constitution of an atom . . . is such as to render it, so far as we can judge, independent of all the dangers arising from the struggle for existence' (*Encyclopaedia Britannica*, Vol. 3, pp.43-45;49). Maxwell is deliberately drawing attention to the stability and permanence of contemporary physical conceptions. *Middlemarch* is about the struggle for existence, about lives in time, courtship, marriage, birth and death; it is a historical novel in which human atoms change with a changing environment. George Eliot may use physics for a model of the speculative imagination but her fictional laws are evolutionary: complexity of relations, repetition with variation, progression and continued divergence – 'the strange irregular rhythm of life' (Henry James, 'The Art of Fiction', *Longman's Magazine*, Vol. 4, 1884, p.515.)

> Old provincial society had its share of this subtle movement: had not only its striking downfalls, its brilliant young professional dandies who ended by living up an entry with a drab and six children for their

establishment, but also those less marked vicissitudes which are constantly shifting the boundaries of social intercourse, and begetting new consciousness of interdependence. Some slipped a little downwards, some got higher footing: people denied aspirates, gained wealth, and fastidious gentlemen stood for boroughs; some were caught in political currents, some in ecclesiastical, and perhaps found themselves surprisingly grouped in consequence; while a few personages or families that stood with rocky firmness amid all this fluctuation, were slowly presenting new aspects in spite of solidity, and altering with the double change of self and beholder. Municipal town and rural parish gradually made fresh threads of connection – gradually, as the old stocking gave way to the savings-bank, and the worship of the solar guinea became extinct; while squires and baronets, and even lords who had once lived blamelessly afar from the civic mind, gathered the faultiness of further acquaintanceship. Settlers, too, came from distant counties, some with an alarming novelty of skill, others with an offensive advantage in cunning.

George Eliot, *Middlemarch* (1871–72), Chapter 11,
Vol. 1, pp.164–65.

Advantage, we suddenly realise, is a technical term for this learned and most sophisticated writer. 'How frequently do we hear', Darwin had written, 'of one species of rat taking the place of another species under most different climates!' (*Origin of Species*, p.76). Competition was now biological as well as socio-economic. Notice too Eliot's stress on gradual change; 'a slow preparation of effects', she had called it in the preceding paragraph. Though 'gradualism' is in many ways typically Victorian, we should remember that Lamarck's version of biological evolution in 1809 had required countless generations in which to take effect; this he proposed at a time when geologists were still divided into catastrophists and uniformitarians, mostly the former. He was a uniformitarian before the word had even been coined, in Whewell's fascinating review of the second volume of Lyell's *Principles*, where Whewell was even more dismissive of Lamarck's transmutation of species over 'an indefinite number of generations' than Lyell had been. He made fun of 'the gradual working of the natural tendencies of the animals themselves' by invoking creatures 'incessantly urged by feelings of endowments unpossessed, of the same kind with an oyster's "sentiment" of the want of a head, or a snail's of the need of a back-bone' (*Quarterly Review*, Vol. 47, 1832, pp.113-15; 126). Darwin rejected many of Lamarck's ideas, such as the spontaneous generation of life, but he undoubtedly believed in gradual development. In geology Darwin stressed slow and gradual change more than Lyell; in biology he allowed for the possibility of sudden changes or leaps but insisted on 'a *working* theory of a slow and gradual change by means of the effective causes that could be studied in the present: variation, heredity, rates of reproduction, the struggle for existence, geographical distribution' (N.C. Gillespie, *Charles Darwin and the Problem of Creation* (1979), p.62).

'Light will be thrown on the origin of man and his history', Darwin had written. In Hardy's early novel, *A Pair of Blue Eyes*, one heavily significant light is thrown by palaeontology. As Henry Knight hangs desperately on the Cliff without a Name, he has a vision of human kind without dignity or special place in the world.

> By one of those familiar conjunctions in which the inanimate world baits the mind of man when he pauses in moments of suspense, opposite Knight's eyes was an imbedded fossil, standing forth in low relief from the rock. It was a creature with eyes. The eyes, dead and turned to stone, were even now regarding him. It was one of the early crustaceans called Trilobites. Separated by millions of years in their lives, Knight and this underling seemed to have met in their [place of] death. It was the single instance within reach of his vision of anything that had ever been alive and had a body to save, as he himself had now.
>
> The creature represented but a low type of animal existence, for never in their vernal years had the plains

indicated by those numberless slaty layers been traversed by an intelligence worthy of the name. Zoophytes, mollusca, shell-fish, were the highest development of those ancient dates. The immense lapses of time each formation represented had known nothing of the dignity of man. They were grand times but they were mean times too, and mean were their relics. He was to be with the small in his death. . . .
Time closed up like a fan before him.

> Thomas Hardy, *A Pair of Blue Eyes* (1873),
> Chapter 22, Vol. 2, pp.182-84.

Hardy might almost be carrying on a debate with Buckland, who had chosen 'nearly four hundred microscopic lenses set side by side, in the compound eye of a fossil Trilobite' as a supreme example of Creative Intelligence, N.A. Rupke tells us; it was a 'perfect' creature in its adaptation to its environment. But Knight's is an obstinately human scale: when his own life is at stake, 'such an experiment in killing might have been practised on some less developed life' (Ibid, pp.191-92).

Later novels continue this emphasis. The evolution of human intelligence and consciousness was a tragic accident, bringing awareness of our fate. In *The Return of the Native* (1878) Clym Yeobright's face 'showed that thought is a disease of flesh, and indirectly bore evidence that ideal physical beauty is incompatible with growth of fellow-feeling and a full sense of the coil of things' (Book 2, Chapter 6). Hamlet by 'this mortal coil' meant the tumult and bustle of life. To this Hardy adds the sense of the coiling of snares, internally as well as externally, for Darwinism went beyond the simple view that we are trapped by our circumstances. We are, so to speak, tuned by them, but tuned in a way that makes us positively responsive to our fate.

> Man can act only on external and visible characters; nature cares nothing for appearances, except in so far as they may be useful to any being. She can act on every internal organ, on every shade of constitutional difference, on the whole machinery of life. . . .

It may be said that natural selection is daily and hourly scrutinising, throughout the world, every variation, even the slightest; rejecting that which is bad, preserving and adding up all that is good; silently and insensibly working, whenever and wherever opportunity offers, at the improvement of each organic being in relation to its organic and inorganic conditions of life.

Charles Darwin, *Origin of Species* (1859), Chapter 4, pp.83-84.

In later novels Hardy has the same view of the biologically active universe as Darwin, but his values are very different. Men and women are central; he is anthropocentric in a way that Darwin deliberately avoided being in the *Origin of Species*.

It was a typical summer evening of June, the atmosphere being in such delicate equilibrium and so transmissive that inanimate objects seemed endowed with two or three senses, if not five. There was no distinction between the near and the far, and an auditor felt close to everything within the horizon. The soundlessness impressed her as a positive entity rather than as the mere negation of noise. It was broken by the notes of a harp. . . .

To speak absolutely, both instrument and execution were poor; but the relative is all, and as she listened Tess, like a fascinated bird, could not leave the spot. Far from leaving she drew up towards the performer, keeping behind the hedge that he might not guess her presence.

The outskirt of the garden in which Tess found herself had been left uncultivated for some years, and was now damp and rank with juicy grass which sent up mists of pollen at a touch; and with tall blooming weeds emitting offensive smells – weeds whose red and yellow and purple hues formed a polychrome as dazzling as that of cultivated flowers. She went stealthily as a cat through this profusion of growth, gathering cuckoo spittle on her skirts, cracking snails that were underfoot, staining her hands with thistle-milk and slug-slime, and rubbing off upon her naked arms sticky blights which, though snow-white on the apple-tree trunks, made blood-red stains upon her skin; thus she drew quite near to Clare, still unobserved by him.

Tess was conscious of neither time nor space. The exaltation which she had described as being producible at will by gazing at a star, came now without any determination of hers; she undulated upon the thin notes as upon billows, and their harmonies passed like breezes through her, bringing tears into her eyes. The floating pollen seemed to be his notes made visible, and the dampness of the garden the weeping of the garden's sensibility. Though near nightfall, the rank-smelling weed flowers glowed as if they would not close for intentness, and the waves of colour mixed with the waves of sound.

Thomas Hardy, *Tess of the d'Urbervilles* (1891),
Chapter 19, Vol. 1, pp.244-46.

Fertilising pollen is now included in the old physical analogy between light and sound. Tess's courtship begins with her trembling in an instinctual breeze; her Romantic 'exaltation' lacks both the asceticism and the delicate sensuality of Keats's 'Bright star' sonnet. Tess has neither human steadfastness nor 'sweet unrest' as she succumbs to the basic biological drive to procreate. Hardy is deliberately revising Romantic experience and values. Where, he asks, did Wordsworth get his authority for speaking of 'Nature's holy plan'? Tess is embarking on yet another tragic course. But Hardy is revising Romanticism for a biological scheme that to him is obnoxiously true. What he cannot accept is Darwin's overall assessment and sense of values.

All that we can do, is to keep steadily in mind that each organic being is striving to increase at a geometrical ratio; that each at some period of its life, during some season of the year, during each generation or at intervals, has to struggle for life, and to suffer great destruction. When we reflect on this struggle, we may console ourselves with the full belief, that the war of nature is not incessant, that no fear is felt, that death is generally prompt, and that the vigorous, the healthy, and the happy survive and multiply.

Charles Darwin, *Origin of Species*, Chapter 3, pp.78-79.

Darwin actually believed that happiness had a survival value and in later years would drolly maintain that novels should be made to end happily by law – in which case statute law would reflect the operation of natural law, and one great problem of literary realism be solved!

According to my judgment happiness decidedly prevails, though this would be very difficult to prove. If the truth of this conclusion be granted it harmonises well with the effects which we might expect from natural selection. If all the individuals of any species were to suffer to an extreme degree they would neglect to propagate their kind; but we have no reason to believe that this has ever or at least often occurred. . . .

Now an animal may be led to pursue that course of action which is the most beneficial to the species by suffering, such as pain, hunger, thirst and fear, – or by pleasure, as in eating and drinking and in the propagation of the species &c., or by both means combined as in the search for food. . . . Hence it has come to pass that most or all sentient beings have been developed in such a manner through natural selection that pleasurable sensations serve as their habitual guides. . . . The sum of such pleasures as these, which are habitual or frequently recurrent, give, as I can hardly doubt, to most sentient beings an excess of happiness over misery, although many occasionally suffer much.

Charles Darwin, *Autobiographies* (1974), pp.51-52; 83.

Hardy, like Darwin, responded with sensuous pleasure to natural life in all its diversity.

> When the Present has latched its postern behind my
>   tremulous stay,
> And the May month flaps its glad green leaves like
>   wings,
> Delicate-filmed as new-spun silk, will the neighbours
>   say,
> 'He was a man who used to notice such things'?

Thomas Hardy 'Afterwards' (1917), stanza 1.

There is no doubt about the answer to such questions. Passage after passage shows his response to joy in life, from the timid community of zoophytes, plant-like water creatures, expressing 'gladness' when a stray ray of sun warms their little aquarium world in *A Pair of Blue Eyes* to the rising animation of Egdon Heath in *The Return of the Native* when the month of March arrives. But human joy hardly appears to have survival value. It exists: playing and singing 'fortissimy' with the Mellstock Quire in *Under the Greenwood Tree*, sheep-shearing in *Far From the Madding Crowd*, cider-making by 'Autumn's very brother' in *The Woodlanders*, lighting winter fires on Egdon Heath – 'a spontaneous, Promethean rebelliousness against the fiat that this recurrent season shall bring foul times, cold darkness, misery and death . . . .' (*The Return of the Native* (1878), Book 1, Chapter 3).

But these are rural communities where happiness has found its last refuge – amongst those who have not attained a perfect insight into the true conditions of existence, Hardy told us in an essay on 'The Dorsetshire Labourer' (*Longman's Magazine*, 1883). 'That old-fashioned revelling in the general situation grows less and less possible as we uncover the defects of natural laws, and see the quandary that man is in by their operation' (*Return of the Native* (1878), Book 3, Chapter 1). Darwin's excess of happiness over misery, the balance struck by a man who enjoyed ill health and a good family life, did not recommend itself to Hardy in this mood. His view is shared by Elizabeth Jane, a character who had, by chance, survived.

Her experience had been of a kind to teach her, rightly or wrongly, that the doubtful honour of a brief transit through a sorry world hardly called for effusiveness, even when the path was suddenly irradiated at some half-way point by daybeams rich as hers. But her strong sense that neither she nor any human being deserved less than was given, did not blind her to the fact that there were others receiving less who had deserved much more. And in being forced to class herself among the fortunate she did not cease to wonder at the persistence of the unforeseen, when the one to whom such unbroken tranquillity had been accorded in the adult stage was she whose youth had seemed to teach that happiness was but the occasional episode in a general drama of pain.

Thomas Hardy, *The Mayor of Casterbridge* (1886), Chapter 45, Vol. 2, p.312.

Life in the Future

In his epilogue to *Yeast* (1848) Kingsley had reiterated Carlyle's belief that traditional systems of thought were breaking up like ice in a thaw and that new artistic forms were required. Not all his contemporaries reacted with the same imaginative ebullience as Kingsley, however. In Richard Jefferies' *After London* (1885) the democratic aggression of thorns and brambles Whewell had envisaged turns London into a choked and putrid swamp. Similarly, as a young science student in the 1880s H.G. Wells speculated that our remote descendents might be quite alien to us. *The Time Machine* (1895) presents humanity evolved into two degenerate species, Eloi and Morlocks; the harmless, delicate Eloi and the fearsome, subterranean Morlocks came from two nineteenth-century types – aesthetic and pleasure-loving, or puritan and mechanically industrious. In another of his future fantasies Wells eliminates the element of evolutionary chance and shows what could be made of intelligent life in the universe. The vision is no less disconcerting.

All of them had a grotesque and disquieting suggestion of an insect that has somehow contrived to mock humanity; but all seemed to present an incredible exaggeration of some particular feature: one had a vast right fore-limb, an enormous antennal arm, as it were; one seemed all leg, poised, as it were, on stilts; another protruded the edge of his face-mask into a nose-like organ that made him startlingly human until one saw his expressionless gaping mouth. . . . One distortion was particularly conspicuous. There were several brain cases distended like bladders to a huge size, with the face mask reduced to quite small proportions.

H.G. Wells, *The First Men in the Moon* (1901),
Chapter 24, pp.295-96.

These moon-dwellers, Selenites, are certainly adapted to their conditions in a dystopian society, from young ones in jars from which only the fore-limbs protrude as they are turned into specialist machine-minders to the ruler of all, the vast and glowing brain called the Grand Lunar.

Wells' satiric fantasy of bio-engineering reveals a fear of rigid, 'scientific' analyses and their Promethean extensions into human life. The scientist who observes the Selenites, Cavor, is himself portrayed as machine-like and single-minded; like a more subtle and accomplished Frankenstein, he sees everything through the lens of his own obsessions and does not care for the consequences. We trespass here on the nineteenth-century fear of technology, expressed as early as 1829 in Carlyle's *Edinburgh Review* essay 'Signs of the Times' and reinforced by Ruskin in Volume 2 of *The Stones of Venice* (1853, Chapter 6), where he writes of the 'degradation of the operative into a machine' and the division of men, not labour. On a theoretical level, however, we can find John Herschel comparing atoms to 'manufactured articles, on account of their uniformity', and Maxwell using this multiplied identity as an argument for divine creation: '. . . a number of exactly similar things cannot be each of them eternal and self-existent, and must therefore have been made' (*Encyclopaedia Britannica*, Vol. 3, p.49). Biology inspired Wells to counter-arguments that support Bergson's analysis of the nature of comedy in *Le Rire* (1900) – it arises from the denial of the natural and instinctive, the intellectual mechanising of a reality that is never abstract, but always organic and changing, ever individual and resistant to imposition. Wells made his objections quite explicit in a wide-ranging essay.

> In a sentence it is, *All being is unique*, or, nothing is strictly like anything else. It implies, therefore, that we only arrive at the idea of similar beings by an unconscious or deliberate disregard of an infinity of small differences. . . . Human reason, in the light of what is being advanced, appears as a convenient organic process . . . and it may – though the presumption is against such a view – take us away from, rather than towards, the absolute truth of things. The *raison d'être* of a man's mind is to avoid danger and get food – so the naturalists tell us. His reasoning powers are about as much a truth-seeking tool as the snout of a pig, and he may as well try to get to the bottom of things by them as a mole might by burrowing. . . .
>
> The most indisputable corollary of the rediscovery is the destruction of the atomic theory. There is absolutely no ground in human experience for a presumption of similar atoms, the mental entanglement that created one being now unravelled, and similarly the certainty of all the so-called laws of physics and chemistry is now assailable. . . .
>
> The period of darkest ignorance, when men turned their backs on nature and believed in mystic numbers, has long passed away; even the skulls of the schoolmen have rotted to dust by this time, and their books are in tatters. The work of Darwin and Wallace was the clear assertion of the uniqueness of living things . . . .
>
> H.G. Wells, 'The Rediscovery of the Unique',
> *Fortnightly Review*, Vol. 56, 1891, pp.106-109; 111.

This essay as a whole is as tendentious as it could be. No one, for instance, was more aware than Maxwell that physical models were themselves subject to mutation, merely provisional. Relativity had entered the physical sciences two generations before with the major generalisations of thermodynamics, which relate to change that can only be described statistically, precisely because individual occurrences are too various to be determined or described in detail. Nevertheless, there is no doubt about the influence that Wells attributed to biology above all, to the importance of minute, successful variations in living organisms and to the insensible gradations between them, vertically and horizontally – through time and across space. And was the human mind, then, a 'disease of flesh', as Hardy had proclaimed, or was it an adaptive instrument of discovery in living and changing experience?

3 Psychology, Anatomy, Physiology

Mind and Matter

Psychology was once in the cool hands of the philosophers. In his *Discourse on the Method* (1637), Descartes had stated a famous principle: 'I observed that this truth, *I think, therefore I am*, was so solid and certain that all the most extravagant suppositions of the sceptics were unable to upset it.' *I think* must be broadly construed. The subjective awareness of an individual mind is the most certain reality, rather than any kind of material existence outside such a consciousness. Even the body can be regarded as no more than a complicated machine, an automaton – an assertion that became 'a more or less scandalous commonplace supported on the one hand by enormous advances in physiology and biochemistry, and on the other hand by equally enormous developments in machinery' (A. Flew, *An Introduction to Western Philosophy* (1971), pp.280-95). This 'Cartesian dualism', or sharp distinction between mind and body, became a main frame of reference for Western philosophers and psychologists into this century. Though the philosopher Gilbert Ryle in *The Concept of Mind* (1949) argues against 'the ghost in the machine', it can be very useful as an organising concept when considering what was often called 'mental philosophy' or 'science of mind' well into the nineteenth century. The word *psychology* was not really established as the name of the science until about mid-century.

Coleridge was typically Romantic in objecting to the way in which the 'intellect and moral being' had been 'conjured within the magic circle of mechanical forces, and controlled by mathematical formulae' (*Fraser's Magazine*, Vol. 12, 1835, p.625). He praised 'the increasingly dynamic spirit of the physical sciences'.

99

It is not Chemistry alone that will be indebted to the genius of Davy, Oersted, and their compeers: and not as the founder of physiology and philosophic anatomy alone, will mankind love and revere the name of John Hunter. ... nothing would be more easy than so to construct the paper, ink, printed capitals, and the like, of a printed disquisition on the eye, or the muscles and cellular texture (that is, the flesh) of the human body, as to bring together every one of the sensible and ponderable stuffs or elements, that are sensuously perceived in the eye itself, or in the flesh itself. Carbon and nitrogen, oxygen and hydrogen, sulphur, phosphorus, and one or two metals and metallic bases, constitute the whole. It cannot be these, therefore, that we mean by an eye, by our body. But perhaps it may be a particular combination of these? Now here comes a question: In this term do you or do you not include the principle, the operating cause, of the combination? If not, then detach this eye from the body. Look steadily at it – as it might lie on the marble slab of a dissecting room. ... Is this cold jelly *the light of the body*? ...

But perhaps the material particles possess [a] combining power by inherent reciprocal attractions, repulsions, and elective affinities; and are themselves the joint artists of their own combinations? I will not reply, though well I might, that this would be to solve one problem by another, and merely to shift the mystery. It will be sufficient to remind the thoughtful querist, that even herein consists the essential difference, the contra-distinction, of an organ from a machine; that not only the characteristic shape is evolved from the invisible central power, but the material mass itself is acquired by assimilation. The germinal power of the plant transmutes the fixed air and the elementary base of water into grass or leaves; and on these the organific principle in the ox or the elephant exercises an alchemy still more stupendous. As the unseen agency weaves its magic eddies, the foliage becomes indifferently the bone and its marrow, the pulpy brain, or the solid ivory. That what you see is blood, is flesh, is itself the work, or shall I say, the translucence, of the invisible energy, ...

S.T. Coleridge, *Aids to Reflection* (1825), 9th edn, 1861, pp.330-33.

In 'The Devil and the Lady' the young Tennyson was still using mechanical analogies: 'Each Being is a world within himself, / A complicated Engine, whose main springs / Are circumstance and habit' (I.iv.62-64). But 'Armageddon' ends with a fully organic vision.

> The clear stars
> Shone out with keen yet fixed intensity,
> All-silence, looking steadfast consciousness
> Upon the dark and windy waste of Earth.
> There was a beating in the atmosphere,
> An indefinable pulsation,
> Inaudible to outward sense, but felt
> Through the deep heart of every living thing,
> As if the great soul of the Universe
> Heaved with tumultuous throbbings on the vast
> Suspense of some grand issue.

Lord Tennyson, 'Armageddon' (c.1824), Part 4, ll.24-34, ed. Ricks, p.74.

Strange Powers of Mind

The psychological aspects of literature in the early part of the nineteenth century are well known. Coleridge published 'Kubla Khan' in 1816, with a note that he had done so 'rather as a psychological curiosity, than on the ground of any supposed *poetic* merits'. It had, he said, been composed in 'a sort of Reverie brought on by two grains of Opium'. Several of his other poems display more normal, but still wonderful, powers and processes of human thought. 'Frost at Midnight' is a waking reverie – on his childhood and that of his infant son, a film of soot ('Whose puny flaps and freaks the idling Spirit / By its own moods interprets'), and the more indefinable 'secret ministry of frost' that hangs up the eaves drops 'in silent icicles, / Quietly shining to the quiet Moon' (ll.20-21; 73-74). This last beautiful image is a perfect example of the mind's symbol-making power according to his own definition, 'the translucence of the eternal through and in the temporal' (*S.T. Coleridge: Poems*, ed. J. Beer (1974), pp.xxvi-xxix; 163-64).

Coleridge's most remarkable successor was Thomas De Quincey, whose *Confessions of an English Opium Eater* was published in the *London Magazine* for 1821. Its third section, 'The Pains of Opium', is more than a case study of addiction. It can be regarded, in those days before psychology was organised as a science, as a pioneering study of the activity of the unconscious mind in dreams, combined with a dazzling attempt to recreate them in language. He tells first of 'the re-awakening of a state of eye oftentimes incident to childhood', when phantoms are painted, 'as it were, upon the darkness'.

> The minutest incidents of childhood, or forgotten scenes of later years, were often revived: I could not be said to recollect them; for, if I had been told of them when waking, I should not have been able to acknowledge them as parts of my past experience. . . . I feel assured, that there is no such thing as ultimate *forgetting*; traces once impressed upon the memory are indestructible; a thousand accidents may and will interpose a veil between our present consciousness and the secret inscriptions on the mind. Accidents of the same sort will also rend away this veil. But alike, whether veiled or unveiled, the inscription remains for ever; . . . .

> Thomas De Quincey, *Confessions of an English Opium Eater* (1821), 1883 edn pp.257-61.

In those early decades of the century, before shades of the prison house had begun to close upon the science of mind as practised by inspired amateurs, De Quincey's explanations of dreaming ranged from the physiological to the spiritual.

In the early stages of the malady, the splendours of my dreams were indeed chiefly architectural: and I beheld such pomp of cities and palaces as never yet was beheld by the waking eye, unless in the clouds. . . . To my architecture succeeded dreams of lakes and silvery expanses of water: these haunted me so much, that I feared that some dropsical state or tendency of the brain might thus be making itself (to use a metaphysical word) *objective*; and that the sentient organ might be *projecting* itself as its own object.

Ibid, pp.264-65.

The machinery for dreaming planted in the human brain was not planted for nothing. That faculty, in alliance with the mystery of darkness, is the one great tube through which man communicates with the shadowy. And the dreaming organ, in connection with the heart, the eye, and the ear, compose the magnificent apparatus which forces the infinite into the chambers of a human brain, and throws dark reflections from eternities below all life upon the mirrors of [*later*, that mysterious *camera obscura* –] the sleeping mind.

Thomas De Quincey, 'Suspiria de Profundis', *Blackwood's Magazine*, Vol. 57, 1845, p.270.

The second quotation provides a kind of explanation of the trance experiences Tennyson evokes in poems like 'Armageddon' and Section 95 of *In Memoriam*.

The earliest recorded use of *sub-conscious* (*OED*, 1823) is taken, in an adverbial form, from De Quincey's essay on style: 'Whilst the finest models of style exist, and sub-consciously operate effectively as sources of delight . . . .' Through De Quincey's own impassioned, musical prose we sympathise with his imaginative life, itself intimately dependent upon his dreams and reveries. These he attributes to his boyhood sufferings especially, to 'those *encaustic* records which in the mighty furnaces of London life had been burnt into the undying memory of the fierce action of misery' (*Confessions of an English Opium Eater*, p.232). Their creative consequences are pithily expressed by a German author De Quincey introduced to the British public in 1821, J.P.F. Richter: 'The most powerful thing in the poet, which blows the good and the evil spirit into his works, is precisely the unconscious'; 'The unconscious is really the largest realm in our minds, and just on account of this unconsciousness, the inner Africa, whose unknown boundaries may extend far away' (quoted in L.L. Whyte, *The Unconscious Before Freud* (1960), p.133). The 'palimpsest of the human brain' (*Blackwood's Magazine*, Vol. 57, pp.742–43) was not a slate that could be wiped clean; it was a parchment that could be inscribed again and again, even though it preserved hidden layer after layer of experience – never erased, and sometimes released in terrible dreams. His metaphor of the palimpsest proved popular, not only with Elizabeth Browning (*Aurora Leigh*, Book 1, l.826) but also with psychologists like G.H. Lewes, James Sully and Sigmund Freud.

> Southern Asia, in general, is the seat of awful images and associations. As the cradle of the human race, if on no other ground, it would alone have a dim, reverential feeling connected with it. But there are other reasons. No man can pretend that the wild, barbarous, and capricious superstitions of Africa, or of savage tribes elsewhere, affect him in the way that he is affected by the ancient, monumental, cruel, and elaborate religions of Hindostan. The mere antiquity of Asiatic things, of their institutions, histories, above all, of their mythologies, &c. is so impressive, that to me the vast age of the race and name overpowers the sense of youth in the individual. A young Chinese seems to me an antediluvian man renewed. Even Englishmen, though not bred in any knowledge of such institutions, cannot but shudder at the mystic sublimity of *castes* that have flowed apart, and refused to mix, through such immemorial tracts of time; . . . South-eastern Asia is, and has been for thousands of years, the part of the earth most swarming with human life; . . . . Man is a weed in those regions. . . . All this, and much more than I can say, the reader must enter into, before he can comprehend the unimaginable horror which these

dreams of Oriental imagery and mythological tortures impressed upon me. Under the connecting feeling of tropical heat and vertical sunlights, I brought together all creatures, birds, beasts, reptiles, all trees and plants, usages and appearances, that are found in all tropical regions, and assembled them together in China or Hindostan. From kindred feelings, I soon brought Egypt and her gods under the same law. I was stared at, hooted at, grinned at, chattered at, by monkeys, by paroquets, by cockatoos. I ran into pagodas, and was fixed for centuries at the summit, or in secret rooms; I was the idol; I was the priest; I was worshipped; I was sacrificed. I fled from the wrath of Brama through all the forests of Asia: Vishnu hated me: Seeva laid wait for me. I came suddenly upon Isis and Osiris: I had done a deed, they said, which the ibis and the crocodile trembled at. Thousands of years I lived and was buried in stone coffins, with mummies and sphinxes, in narrow chambers at the heart of eternal pyramids. I was kissed, with cancerous kisses, by crocodiles, and was laid, confounded with all unutterable abortions, amongst reeds and Nilotic mud.

> Thomas De Quincey, *Confessions of an English Opium Eater* (1821), 1883 edn, pp.266-68.

De Quincey seems to be establishing what one might call a school of morbid anthropology some eighty years before Conrad's *Lord Jim*!

The interest in abnormal psychology continued in Browning's dramatic monologues like 'Porphyria's Lover' and 'Soliloquy of the Spanish Cloister'. In his *Men and Women* (1855) occurs a poem that portrays a sceptical man of science who encounters Lazarus, risen from the dead.

> Tis but a case of mania – subinduced
> By epilepsy, at the turning point
> Of trance prolonged unduly some three days:

> Robert Browning, 'An Epistle containing the Strange Medical Experience of Karshish, the Arab Physician' (1855), ll.79-81.

More recent science (though Karshish is a nineteenth-century Rationalist in some ways figures in one of the world's first detective stories, *The Moonstone*. Wilkie Collins exploits contemporary writings upon unconscious behaviour, in order to provide, eventually, a rational explanation for the mysterious theft at the centre of the novel's plot. Franklin Blake in a 'morbidly sensitive nervous condition', apprehensive that the moonstone would be stolen by Hindu conspirators, had unknowingly removed it to a place of safety whilst under the influence of opium. Next day he had forgotten his action altogether. Doctor Jennings realised the truth and was certain that he could make Blake repeat the deed.

> 'Observe, Mr. Blake, before you begin, that I am referring you to one of the greatest of English physiologists. The book in your hand is Doctor Elliotson's *Human Physiology* [1835]; and the case which the doctor cites rests on the well-known authority of Mr. Combe.' . . .
>
> 'Dr. Abel informed me', says Mr. Combe, 'of an Irish porter to a warehouse, who forgot, when sober, what he had done when drunk; but, being drunk, again recollected the transactions of his former state of intoxication. On one occasion, being drunk, he had lost a parcel of some value, and in his sober moments could give no account of it. Next time he was intoxicated, he recollected that he had left the parcel at a certain house, and there being no address on it, it had remained there safely, and was got on his calling for it.'
>
> Wilkie Collins, *The Moonstone* in *All the Year Round*, Vol. 20, 1868, p.100.

This is a direct reference to a book by a friend of Collins and of Charles Dickens. John Elliotson had been professor of medicine at University College Hospital, but was forced to resign in 1838 because of his interest in mesmerism (or 'animal magnetism', or hypnotism: *OED*, 1802) and other aspects of 'human nature in a new state'. He then lived by private practice and by authorship.

There is a clear echo of Collins in the third chapter of Dickens' last, unfinished novel, *Edwin Drood* (1870), when he writes of 'two states of consciousness which never clash, but each of which pursues its separate course as though it were continuous instead of broken (thus if I hide my watch when drunk, I must be drunk again before I can remember where)'. This novel, however, makes such double states of being a structural principle of the whole. It begins in hallucination, as the fractured personality of Edwin Drood is shown recovering from an opium bout, overlaying the square tower of an English cathedral with the spike 'set up by the Sultan's orders for the impaling of a horde of Turkish robbers' and invading a calm English cathedral town with a cruel, beautiful, orgiastic procession from the Orient. The power of this novel was not to lie in the mechanical details of a mystery plot, but, according to Dickens' daughter, in 'the psychological description the murderer gives us of his temptations, temperament, and character, as if told by another' (*Edwin Drood*, ed. M. Cardwell (1972), p.xx).

The line of ancestry through De Quincey's *Confessions* to 'Kubla Khan', with its ambiguous, daemonic forces, is clear but so is the influence of contemporary scientific interest in double states of being. The 'sensation novel' of the 1860s was a natural vehicle for such psychological phenomena, supplemented to some degree with scientific features. Collins proved to be particularly adept. The memorable character Count Fosco in *The Woman in White*, which was serialised in Dickens' *All the Year Round* between November 1859 and August 1860, boasts of his strange power of mind over others – aided occasionally by chemistry; for mind, which rules the world, is ruled by the body, which lies at the mercy of the Chemist! In *Armadale*, serialised in the *Cornhill Magazine* from November 1864 to June 1866, Collins cleverly compares the fatalistic and the scientifically rational explanations of a complex dream. There is also an impressive description of a private sanatorium in this novel, but this relates to the social aspects of scientific practice. As Oscar Wilde said of R.L. Stevenson's *The Strange Case of Dr. Jekyll and Mr. Hyde* (1886), 'the transformation of Dr. Jekyll reads dangerously like an experiment out of the *Lancet*' ('Decay of Lying', p.38).

The Body and Its Brain

The ancient science of anatomy (*OED*, 1398) deals with the physical structure of plants and animals. In the early nineteenth century the stealing of human bodies for dissection was notorious. The 'resurrectionists' Burke and Hare were tried for murder of living victims, the former leaving his name to the language when he was executed in 1829: 'Burke him, . . . Burke Hare too!' was cried at the scaffold.

> The reverend gentleman recoiled two or three paces, and saw before him a couple of ruffians, who were preparing to renew the attack, but whom, with two swings of his bamboo, he laid with cracked sconces on the earth, where he proceeded to deal with them like corn beneath the flail of the thresher. . . . 'Confess speedily, villain; are you simple thief, or would you have manufactured me into a subject, for the benefit of science? Ay, miscreant caitiff, you would have made me a subject for science, would you? You are a schoolmaster abroad, are you? You are marching with a detachment of the march of mind, are you? You are a member of the Steam Intellect Society, are you? You swear by the learned friend, do you?

> T.L. Peacock, *Crotchet Castle* (1831), Chapter 8.

Peacock's satire takes in the work of Henry Brougham and the Society for the Diffusion of Useful Knowledge (the 'Sixpenny Science Company'), founded in 1826. For him these were all aspects of the cult of progress, 'the march of mind', to be deplored. Peacock's satire also takes in physiology (*OED*, 1597), the study of the functioning of organs. The aptly named Mr Henbane has poisoned and revived a frog eleven times, like B.C. Brodie, surgeon and toxicologist, who was known to have poisoned and revived a cat (M. Butler, *Peacock Displayed* (1979), pp.184; 242-46). The cat lived, but Mr Henbane's twelfth experiment was a failure (*Crotchet Castle*, Chapter 6).

Robert Chambers brought out the popular simplistic view of 'what all observation teaches, that mental phenomena flow directly from the brain', and boldly asserted 'the absolute identity of the brain with a galvanic battery' (*Vestiges*, pp.332; 334). Chambers was relying upon physiological experiments of the time; and indeed a major scientist like John Herschel was, as we have seen, prepared to associate the operations of the brain with electricity – with hypothetical matters safe in a footnote.

> If the brain be an electric pile, constantly in action, it may be conceived to discharge itself at regular intervals, when the tension of the electricity developed reaches a certain point, along the nerves which communicate with the heart, and thus to excite the pulsations of that organ.

> John Herschel, *A Preliminary Discourse* (1831), 1832 edn, p.343.

Blatantly or cautiously put, however, such analogies from physics can be made to press hard upon the free life of the mind, especially the mind responding to the 'indefinable pulsation' of the 'great soul of the Universe'. Tennyson's later reading in P.M. Roget's *Animal and Vegetable Physiology* (1834) would have reinforced the opposition he was to display to the materialistic trend in Chambers. Roget, who was a physician by profession, denied a direct connection between matter and mind: 'All that we have been able to accomplish has been to trace the impression from the organ of sense along the communication nerves to the sensorium; beyond this the clue is lost, and we can follow the process no further' (Roget, Vol. 2, p.506). His concern was to retain an 'immaterial agent', to conceive of life as a 'potent spell' (Gliserman, *Victorian Studies*, Vol. 18, pp.289-90). This corresponds with Coleridge's 'unseen agency' weaving its 'magic eddies', the work, or 'translucence, of the invisible energy'. Poet and man of science use metaphors that yoke preternatural and physical powers in the service of religion, to preserve a space for human identity.

> I trust I have not wasted breath:
>   I think we are not wholly brain,
>   Magnetic mockeries; not in vain
> Like Paul with beasts, I fought with Death;

> Not only cunning casts in clay:
>   Let Science prove we are, and then
>   What matters Science unto men,
> At least to me? I would not stay.

Lord Tennyson, *In Memoriam*, Section 120,
eds Shatto and Shaw, p.134.

The physiology of the time had little to say about the data of full human consciousness, still examined by introspective methods and a peculiar province of literature. 'Why is thought being a secretion of brain more wonderful than gravity a property of matter?' is a question Darwin confided to a private notebook in 1838. To Tennyson, reading his dead friend's letters, the answer would have seemed obvious. Gravity is an abstract wonder, utterly impersonal and divorced from spiritual experience.

> So word by word, and line by line,
>   The dead man touch'd me from the past,
>   And all at once it seem'd at last
> The living soul was flash'd on mine,
>
> And mine in this was wound, and whirl'd
>   About empyreal heights of thought,
>   And came on that which is, and caught
> The deep pulsations of the world,

Ibid, Section 95, eds Shatto and Shaw, p.112.

Literature rarely deals with truly detailed physiological investigations such as those of Sir Charles Bell into spinal nerves in the early decades of the century. There was, however, a considerable vogue for a new 'science' called phrenology. It grew out of serious and useful study of the brain but soon developed speciously exact applications to human character, since the human mind was supposed to possess various faculties, which could be assessed by the shape of the skull overlying their separate locations in the brain. The subject was popularised in Britain by George Combe, who founded *The Phrenological Journal and Miscellany*, which ran from 1823–47.

In real life, George Eliot's 'bumps' were read by Combe, who found that she was not fitted to stand alone! In literature Charlotte Brontë described a Radical character as lacking 'the organ of Veneration' and having 'too little of the organs of Benevolence and Ideality' (*Shirley* (1849), Chapter 4). Phrenology could be no more than a parlour game, but it had deterministic implications of the kind we have seen in Tennyson's *The Princess* (1847). George Eliot resorted to its relatively 'static model of the mind' as late as 1863 in *Felix Holt*. In *The Water Babies* of the same year Kingsley bracketed it with the old astrological method of 'casting a nativity' and, ironically hinting at madness, with taking 'the lunars' – actually a way of navigating. Dickens seems just as derisive in *Edwin Drood* (1870): Professional Philanthropists and Pugilists have the same 'development of all those organs which constitute, or attend, a propensity to "pitch into" your fellow creatures' (Chapter 17). The 'science' has now melted into thin air, leaving little more than 'a bump of location' and some fortune-tellers behind.

The 1850s also saw a public craze for table-turning and spirit-rapping. The subject could not fail to attract Bulwer, ever curious and open-minded. He was cautious in his dealings with the American medium Daniel Home, who made his first visit to England in 1855, but borrowed the phenomena of his seances for a short story.

> My eye now rested on the table, and from under the table (which was without cloth or cover – an old mahogany round table) there rose a hand, visible as far as the wrist. It was a hand, seemingly, as much of flesh and blood as my own, but the hand of an aged person – lean, wrinkled, small too – a woman's hand. That hand very softly closed on the two letters that lay on the table; hand and letters both vanished. There then came the same three loud measured knocks I had heard at the bed-head before this extraordinary drama had commenced.
>
> Edward Bulwer, 'The Haunted and the Haunters; or, the House and the Brain' in *Blackwood's Magazine*, Vol. 86, 1859, p.232.

It is not so much these phenomena that interest us after the thrills of an initial reading, but the attempts at a scientific explanation which help pace the story. The narrator may not meet Faraday's standards (Williams, *Michael Faraday*, p.337), but he is not simply credulous.

> 'Whether ... tables walk of their own accord, or fiend-like shapes appear in a magic circle, or bodyless hands rise and remove material objects, or a Thing of Darkness, such as presented itself to me, freeze our blood – still I am persuaded that these are but agencies conveyed, as by electric wires, to my own brain from the brain of another. In some constitutions there is a natural chemistry, and those may produce chemic wonders – in others a natural fluid, call it electricity, and these produce electric wonders. But they differ in this from Normal Science – they are alike objectless, purposeless, puerile, frivolous.

> Ibid, p.236.

Bulwer's scepticism about the results of spiritualism was shared by Peacock, who attacked it in *Gryll Grange* (1860), and Browning, whose Mr Sludge is a rogue.

> Boston's a hole, the herring-pond is wide,
> V-notes are something, liberty still more.
> Besides, is he the only fool in the world?

> Robert Browning, 'Mr Sludge, "The Medium"',
> *Dramatis Personae* (1864), ll.1523-25.

But in all the complex relationships between the science of mind, hypnotism and 'psychic projection' lay a fear of the human brain acting without 'distinct volition', automatically. Bulwer quotes directly from J. Müller's *Physiology of the Senses* in this connection.

> 'But,' I added, in a whisper, terrified by my own question, 'do not physiologists agree in this: namely, that though illusory phantasms may haunt the sane as

well as the insane, the sane know that they are only illusions, and the insane do not?'

'Such a distinction,' answered Faber, 'is far too arbitrary and rigid for more than a very general and qualified acceptance. Müller, indeed, who is, perhaps, the highest authority on such a subject, says, with prudent reserve, "When a person who is not insane sees spectres and believes them to be real, his intellect must be imperfectly exercised." He would, indeed, be a bold physician who maintained that every man who believed he had really seen a ghost was of unsound mind. . . . When I read in the American public journals of "spirit manifestations", in which large numbers of persons of at least the average degree of education, declare that they have actually witnessed various phantasms, . . . and arrive, at once, at the conclusion that they are thus put into direct communication with departed souls, I must assume that they are under an illusion; but I should be utterly unwarranted in supposing that, because they credited that illusion, they were insane.'

E. Bulwer, *A Strange Story*, Chapter 45 in *All the Year Round*, 14 December 1861, p.271.

A full survey of these interconnections, presumably, could not ignore the American periodicals, though a British journal Elliotson wrote for, *The Zoist: A Journal of Cerebral Physiology and Mesmerism* (1843–56) must be a primary source. In literature the subject returned to America with a novel of major importance by Henry James, *The Bostonians* (*Century Magazine*, 1885–86).

Unconscious Cerebration

L.L. Whyte stressed that the 'birth of a relatively trivial term may mark a new orientation in thought' (p.154). He was referring to W.B. Carpenter, who coined the word cerebration (*OED*, 1853) in the phrase 'unconscious cerebration', to describe hidden brain-action which could produce results like those of conscious intellection. To appreciate the full significance of Maggie's actions when she leaves Stephen, we must set them against Carpenter's theory that the mind could work more successfully when left to its own devices: 'Maggie was not conscious of a decision when she turned away from that gloomy averted face, and walked out of the room; it was like an automatic action that fulfils a forgotten intention. What came after? A sense of stairs descended as if in a dream . . .' (George Eliot, *The Mill on the Floss* (1860), Book 6, Chapter 14). The new understanding brought into sharper focus the mysterious and perplexing mental processes that lead up to a decision, increasingly the subject of the novel as it became more psychological and less external in its narrative sequences. Elizabeth Gaskell's *North and South* (1854–55) 'solves' social and industrial problems through the inner life of its heroine, attains narrative resolution by means that are assumed to be only partly conscious.

Elizabeth Gaskell knew Carpenter. George Eliot definitely read Carpenter's *Comparative Physiology* in 1855 and was no doubt aware that he suspected lack of rational control and the influence of '*unconscious* prejudices' formed in childhood. She was, somewhat ambivalently, making Maggie perform an unconscious moral action and may have been challenging linear theories of development that associated human progress with the growth of rationality (Shuttleworth, *George Eliot*, p.75). The whole topic must have been of exceptional interest, if we may judge from the fact that Frances Cobbe contributed two lucid and forward-looking articles to *Macmillan's Magazine* for 1870: 'Unconscious Cerebration: A Psychological Study' and 'Dreams as Illustrations of Unconscious Cerebration'. The first avoids the weirder, more sensational phenomena of mental life; simple instances of our ability to solve problems, or remember, when we give up trying are correlated with the scientific explanations of Carpenter's brain physiology in a lecture he gave at the Royal Institution in 1868. Carpenter had emphasised that the front portion of the brain, the cerebrum, was no longer thought to be 'in direct connection with the organs of sense and the muscular apparatus' but was connected with the sensorium, a part of the brain responsible for receiving and integrating sense-impressions.

As visual changes may take place in the retina of which we are unconscious, either through temporary inactivity of the Sensorium (as in sleep), or through the entire occupation of the attention in some other direction, so may ideational changes take place in the Cerebrum, of which we may be unconscious for want of receptivity on the part of the Sensorium, but of which the results may present themselves to consciousness as ideas elaborated by an automatic process of which we have no cognizance.

> Frances Cobbe, 'Unconscious Cerebration',
> *Macmillan's Magazine*, Vol. 23 (1870), p.35.

Cobbe's conclusions show the state of advanced opinion in the latter part of the century, a movement we can appreciate both in relation to what Dickens had called 'those strange psychological mysteries in ourselves, of which we are all more or less conscious,' which gave authors such 'curious weapons in the armoury of fiction' (Letter to Bulwer, quoted by R.L. Wolff in *Strange Stories and other Explorations in Victorian Fiction* (Boston, 1971), p.289), and also in the light of the rapid development of a more naturalistic, subtly handled psychological novel in the last decades of Victoria's reign.

Can we, or can we *not*, properly speak of our brains as we do of our hearts? Is it more proper to say, 'I invent my dreams,' than it is to say, 'I am beating slowly'? I venture to think the cases are precisely parallel. When our brains perform acts of unconscious cerebration (such as dreams), they act just as our hearts do, *i.e.* involuntarily; and we ought to speak of them as we always do of our hearts, as of organs of our frame, but not our Selves. . . .

But if this presumption be accepted provisionally, and the possibility admitted of its future physiological demonstration, have we, with it, accepted also the Materialist's ordinary conclusion that *we* and our automatically thinking brains are one and indivisible? If the brain can work by itself, have we any reason to believe it ever works *also* under the guidance of something external to itself, which we may describe as the Conscious Self? It seems to me that . . . there are two kinds of action of the brain, the one Automatic, and the other subject to the will of the Conscious Self; just as the actions of a horse are some of them spontaneous and some done under the compulsion of his rider. The first order of actions tend to indicate that the brain 'secretes thought;' the second order (strongly contrasting with the first) show that, beside that automatically working brain, there is another agency in the field under whose control the brain performs a wholly different class of labours.

Frances Cobbe, 'Unconscious Cerebration',
Macmillan's Magazine, Vol. 23 (1870), pp.36-37.

It does indeed. For students of literature Whyte's most striking quotation may be the 'unconscious cerebration of sleep' in *The Aspern Papers* (1888) – not for its own sake, but for its reminder of the most significant novelist in this context of the last two decades of the century, Henry James. The relatively external life of the heroine of *The Bostonians* (1885–86), Verena Tarrant, who in her strange childhood 'had sat on the knees of somnambulists, and been passed from hand to hand by trance-speakers', is a stage on the way to the delicate *realisations* of Lambert Strether in *The Ambassadors* (1903). The 'psychological novel' of the twentieth century has been achieved.

Evolutionary Psychology

Herbert Spencer, a great synthesiser of current ideas, thought that mind had evolved like body, from 'homogeneity to heterogeneity', minute structural changes in the nervous system being products of perpetual interaction between organism and environment. The most complex kinds of mind must have gone through a long history of variation and development, acquired experience becoming innate, and were capable of yet further improvement (*Principles of Psychology* (1855), 1881 edn, Vol. 1, pp.422-26). His science was largely speculative (an unkind joke said that his idea of a tragedy was a hypothesis killed by a fact) but the evolutionary aspects of his psychology typify a subject moving away from the associationist model of a single mind building up all its ideas from sense-experience. Thus G.H. Lewes could write dismissively that the 'flatness' of Dickens's characters, his stereotypes and caricatures, was reminiscent of the behaviour of 'frogs whose brains had been taken out for physiological purposes, and whose actions thenceforth want the distinctive peculiarity of organic action, that of fluctuating spontaneity' (*Fortnightly Review*, Vol. 17, 1872, pp.148-49).

The 'fluctuating spontaneity' Lewes admired can be found in George Eliot's novel *Daniel Deronda* (February–September 1876), which she was composing whilst her companion Lewes was himself writing a book called *The Physical Basis of Mind* (1877). Part of this he published in advance in the newly-established journal *Mind*.

> Experiences which are no longer manifested are said to be stored up in Memory, remaining in the Soul's picture-gallery, visible directly the shutters are opened. We are not conscious of these feelings, yet they exist as latent feelings, and become salient through association. As a metaphorical expression of the familiar facts of Memory this may pass, but it has been converted from a metaphor into an hypothesis, and we are supposed to *have* feelings and ideas, when in fact we have nothing more than a modified *disposition* of the organism – temporary or permanent – which when stimulated will respond in this modified manner. The modification of the organism when permanent becomes hereditary; and its response is then called an instinctive or automatic action. . . .
>
> Picture to yourself this sentient organism incessantly stimulated from without and from within, and adjusting itself in response to such stimulations. In the blending of stimulations, modifying and arresting each

other, there is a fluctuating 'composition of forces', with ever-varying resultants.

Mind, Vol. 2, 1877, p.166.

On the one hand, Lewes is contributing to a journal set up to procure 'a decision of this question as to the scientific standing of psychology' (*Mind*, Vol. 1, 1876, p.3), containing articles by men as important in the history of the subject as Wilhelm Wundt, who founded the first psychological laboratory in 1879. On the other hand, Lewes is presenting George Eliot with a more biological model of human minds in perpetual interaction with the physical environment and with the society that George Eliot herself had described as 'like that wonderful piece of life, the human body, with all its various parts depending on one another, and with a terrible liability to get wrong because of that delicate dependence' (*Blackwood's Magazine*, Vol. 103, 1868, p.4).

Daniel Deronda re-creates the slender and insignificant consciousness of a young woman and her 'blind visions', who nevertheless bore 'onward through the ages the treasure of human affections' (Chapter 11). The characterisation of Gwendolen Harleth is one of the greatest in nineteenth-century fiction, firstly for the 'iridescence of her character – the play of various, nay, contradictory tendencies' (Chapter 4), in her nervous, fluctuating inner being.

> Lo, now, a moment of choice was come. Yet – was it triumph she felt most or terror? Impossible for Gwendolen not to feel some triumph in a tribute to her power at a time when she was first tasting the bitterness of insignificance: again she seemed to be getting a sort of empire over her own life. But how to use it? Here came the terror. Quick, quick, like pictures in a book beaten open with a sense of hurry, came back vividly, yet in fragments, all that she had gone through in relation to Grandcourt – the allurements, the vacillations, the resolve to accede, the final repulsion; the incisive face of that dark-eyed lady with the lovely boy; her own pledge (was it a pledge not to marry him?)

– the new disbelief in the worth of men and things for which that scene of disclosure had been a symbol. That unalterable experience made a vision at which in the first agitated moment, before tempering reflections could suggest themself, her native terror shrank.

George Eliot, *Daniel Deronda* (1876), Chapter 26, ed. G. Handley, Oxford 1984, p.271.

Gwendolen's dilemma about accepting the hand of a rich and powerful man whose real moral duty lies elsewhere, as she knows, is shown in a present swamped by the inrush of memories. George Eliot also believed she must trace the complex interaction between organism and environment as perfectly as the astronomer who 'threads the darkness with strict deduction'; she must 'thread the hidden pathways of feeling and thought which lead up to every moment of action, and to those moments of intense suffering which take the quality of action – like the cry of Prometheus, whose chained anguish seems a greater energy than the sea and sky he invokes and the deity he defies' (Epigraph, Chapter 16). As Gillian Beer has commented, in connection with the imagery from the physical sciences in this novel, the 'idea of endlessness, the *absence* of transformation, is a severe emotional and intellectual strain', when so much is taken up with 'passionate thoughts which can for the most part find no pathway into action' (*Darwin's Plots*, p.188). Yet the subtle movement of dramatised psychology is a second major way in which the novel has been affected by movements of scientific thought in the 1870s. Lewes's 'ever-varying resultants' are seen in the transformations of Gwendolen's anguish and fears.

It seemed more possible that Grandcourt should die: – and yet not likely. The power of tyranny in him seemed a power of living in the presence of any wish that he should die. . . . No! she foresaw him always living, and her own life dominated by him; the 'always' of her young experience not stretching beyond the few immediate years that seemed immeasurably long with her passionate weariness. The thought of his dying

would not subsist: it turned as with a dream-change
into the terror that she should die with his throttling
fingers on her neck avenging that thought. Fantasies
moved within her like ghosts, making no break in her
more acknowledged consciousness and finding no
obstruction in it: dark rays doing their work invisibly in
the broad light.

George Eliot, *Daniel Deronda* (1876), Chapter 48,
pp.563-64.

The rays of physical science doubtless bear their usual
associations of an irresistibly determined fate, but they operate
within a being who has no simply predictable future in
biological terms and, in physiological terms, can only exist in
ever-changing states of 'consensus or unity'.

Just as Darkness is a positive optical sensation very
different from mere privation – just as it replaces the
sensation of Light, blends with it, struggles with it, and
in all respects differs from the *absence* of all optical
sensibility in the skin; so Unconsciousness struggles
with, blends with, and replaces Consciousness in the
organism, and is a positive state in the sentient
organism, not to be confounded with a mere negation
of Sentience; above all, not to be relegated to merely
mechanical processes.

Mind, Vol. 2, 1877, p.160.

In a world of struggle all levels of the human mind seem to have
an adaptive function, a set of responses to our biological need
to organise and manage experience.

4 Anthropology, Ethnology, Philology, Mythology

Race

In his *Researches into the Physical History of Man* (1813, etc.), J.C. Prichard managed to combine a 'firm belief in the *potential* equality of all races' with a theory that the white races had arisen through an innate sexual preference for lighter skin. Adam therefore had been a negro. Scientists like J.F. Blumenbach and the Comte de Buffon, however, decided that Adam and Eve had been white and that other races had arisen by a process of degeneration. Blumenbach thought that the southern slopes of the Caucasus mountains must have been the original home of the human race. Britain's imperial role gave such concepts a formidable impetus; it seemed only too evident that white European descendants of the *Varietas Caucasia* had been irresistibly successful in the struggle for existence against darker races no less than the physical environment. Carlyle's 'Occasional Discourse on the Nigger Question' (*Fraser's Magazine*, December 1849) is often cited in this connection. Carlyle's main concern, however, was with the degenerate state of European civilisation, its mastery of nature gained at the expense of spiritual power. His disciples were many – from Matthew Arnold, whose sonnet 'East and West' laments the change, to Disraeli, who offered an idiosyncratic solution in *Tancred* (1847).

> In conquering sunshine bright
> The man of the bold West now comes array'd;
> He of the mystic East is touched with night.
>
> Matthew Arnold, 'East and West' (1867), ll.12-14.

Early in the novel, the young English nobleman Tancred speaks in 'a voice that comes alike from the brain and from the

121

heart, . . . whose rich and restrained tones exercise, perhaps, on the human frame a stronger spell than even the fascination of the eye, or the bewitching influence of the hand, which is the privilege of the higher races of Asia' (Book 2, Chapter 1). Disillusioned with the condition of England, Tancred decides to penetrate 'the great Asian mystery' by going to the Holy Land. His experiences there culminate in an extraordinary vision on Mount Sinai, when the angel of Arabia, waving 'a sceptre fashioned like a palm tree', explains some of the history of the higher races of Asia and the religious principles they had given to Europe, before it had embarked on its imperialist mission.

> 'That Christendom which thou hast quitted, and over whose expiring attributes thou art a mourner, was a savage forest while the cedars of Lebanon, for countless ages, had built the palaces of mighty kings. Yet in that forest brooded infinite races that were to spread over the globe, and give a new impulse to its ancient life. It was decreed that, when they burst from their wild woods, the Arabian principles should meet them on the threshold of the old world to guide and to civilise them. All had been prepared. The Caesars had conquered the world to place the Laws of Sinai on the throne of the Capitol, and a Galilean Arab advanced and traced on the front of the rude conquerors of the Caesars the subduing symbol of the last development of Arabian principles.'

> Benjamin Disraeli, *Tancred* (1847), Book 4,
> Chapter 6, 1882 edn, p.290.

Disraeli's view of European decay is given a wider historical perspective in *Essai sur l'inégalité des races humaines* (1853–55) by the Comte de Gobineau. Gobineau inquires into the inequality of races in an attempt to discover why ten great civilisations have decayed. Unlike Disraeli, he rejected such causes as the 'decay of religion, fanaticism, corruption of morals, luxury, bad government, despotism', etc. He came to the more biological conclusion that the cause was hybridism: 'The word "degenerate", applied to a people, should and does signify that this people has no longer the intrinsic worth that it formerly possessed, that it no longer has in its veins the same blood, the worth of which has been gradually modified by successive mixtures'. Gobineau was not a simple racist, however: 'I do not question that a good number of Negro chiefs go beyond the common level to which our peasants, or even our decently educated and gifted townspeople can attain, by the force and abundance of their ideas, the high degree of ingenuity of their minds, and the intensity of their active faculties' (quoted by J.R. Baker in *Race* (1974), pp.35-37). This kind of urbane discrimination, together with a satirical view of British society, informs Thackeray's portrait of Miss Swartz, the sentimental and 'rich woolly-haired mulatto from St. Kitt's'.

> 'My sisters say she has diamonds as big as pigeons' eggs,' George said laughing, 'How they must set off her complexion! A perfect illumination it must be when her jewels are on her neck. Her jet-black hair is as curly as Sambo's. I dare say she wore a nose-ring when she went to Court; and with a plume of feathers in her top-knot she would look a perfect Belle Sauvage.'
>
> W.M. Thackeray, *Vanity Fair* (1847–48), Chapter 20, Oxford 1968, pp.244-46.

George Osborne, hardly a paragon himself, rattles away, describing her popularity, but the sting of this episode comes in the tail. The satiric aim suddenly shifts to British values.

> 'I wish they would have loved me,' said Emmy, wistfully. 'They were always very cold to me.'
>
> 'My dear child, they would have loved you if you had two hundred thousand pounds,' George replied. 'That is the way in which they have been brought up. Ours is a ready-money society.'
>
> Ibid.

Gobineau's analysis of decadence is not shared by Thackeray, or Carlyle, or Dickens, or others whose racial stereotypes are carelessly manipulated in order to reveal home truths.

As a character Miss Swartz is no worse than the grotesque

Joseph Sedley, a collector in the East India Company's Civil Service, 'an honourable and lucrative post, as everybody knows' (Chapter 3) – actually a type of plunderer, the nabob, satirised since the eighteenth century. By this time, too, moral disapproval of individual corruption was turning into a general fear that 'all the talk as to the magnificent work of civilising Asia through British influence in India' was 'humbug in practice'. This is from a remarkable first (but only) novel by William Arnold, Matthew's younger brother, called *Oakfield; or, Fellowship in the East*, first published in 1853. A largely autobiographical work, its focus is on the hero's disillusionment with the British in India. Indian scenes and characters are relatively infrequent, though when they are discussed, Arnold makes a painful effort to be fair to something called the 'Asiatic' or 'Native' mind. He praises Indian courage in the Sikh Wars, for instance, but the scale is inevitably tipped against them.

> 'I am sure you exaggerate the lying of the natives, Wykham. You and I could not get on with our servants in every-day life, if truth were not more habitual to them than falsehood. For all you say of their lying, you believe much the greater part of what they say; but allowing that lying is a national vice, and a detestable one, they might retaliate. It is quite conceivable that a good Brahmin, if you can find such a one, shall be as disgusted at our national drunkenness (for judging from our soldiers they will call it a national vice) as we are at their national falsehood. But after all, I grant freely that they are a deplorably inferior race, but I do not see why they should be considered hopelessly so. I know they have souls; and I believe their souls to be as glorious and majestic as yours or mine, though perhaps more terribly hampered.

> W. Arnold, *Oakfield* (2nd ed. 1854), Book 2, Chapter 4, ed. K. Allott (1973), p.141.

Much Victorian literature – whether fantastic, satiric or realistic – is subjective and amateurish where questions of race are touched upon.

Races and Languages

J.F. Blumenbach, the professor of medicine who in 1795 gave the name 'Caucasian' to what some now call Europid stock, was undoubtedly a scientific anthropologist. Like connoisseurs of Labradors, he was well aware that colour is a frail criterion to distinguish species and, though he established a famous collection of human skulls, he was properly cautious about their value in the classification of sub-species or races. Yet he had 'no conception of the evolution of man from apelike ancestors' (Baker, *Race*, p.26). In the first half of the nineteenth century, however, numerous discoveries of flint and bone tools in cave deposits and on ancient geological sites began to make Whewell's joke about *Patriarchosauros* (p.79 above) look less secure. Even though it eventually turned out that human beings of our type inhabited a much later world in time than that of the dinosaurs, there was a growing assurance that the 'antiquity of man' stretched back much further than recorded history. Indeed, the word *prehistoric* was deliberately coined in 1851 by D. Wilson, a hypothesis crystallised out into a necessary descriptive term. In 1857 the remains of 'Neanderthal' man (his skull-cap having great eyebrow ridges like those of an ape, but with a much larger brain capacity) were found near Düsseldorf. Lyell's *Geological Evidences of the Antiquity of Man* and Huxley's *Man's Place in Nature* (both 1863) ensured that theories of descent would be complicated by ideas of, usually, a common animal ancestor, though some (polygenists) thought the various races of mankind came from different ancestors.

Comparative language studies, philology, ran parallel with, or even before, anthropology in certain respects. In a series of lectures given at the Royal Institution in 1861 F. Max Müller proclaimed a single ultimate origin for the world's languages.

> Now, if we consider . . . how Latin . . ., together with Greek, the Celtic, the Teutonic, and Slavonic languages, together likewise with the ancient dialects of India and Persia, points back to an earlier language, the mother, if we may so call it, of the whole Indo-European or Aryan family of speech; if we see how

Hebrew, Arabic, and Syriac, with several minor dialects, are but different impressions of one and the same common type, and must all have flowed from the same source, the original language of the Semitic race; and if we add to these two, the Aryan and Semitic, at least one more well-established class of languages, the Turanian, comprising the dialects of the nomad races scattered over Central and Northern Asia, the Tungusic, Mongolic, Turkic, Samoyedic, and Finnic, all radii from one common centre of speech: if we watch this stream of language rolling on through centuries in three mighty arms, which, before they disappear from our sight in the far distance, clearly show a convergence towards one common source: it would seem, indeed, as if there were an historical life inherent in language, and as if both the will of man and the power of time could tell, if not on its substance, at least on its form.

F.M. Müller, *Lectures on the Science of Language*
(1861), 1871 edn, Vol. 1, pp.35-36.

Müller, like Gobineau, regarded the Aryans as primarily a linguistic group (*OED*, 1847), but one that had formerly lived (cosily united) in Ariana, Central Asia.

The Aryan languages together point to an earlier period of language, when the first ancestors of the Indians, the Persians, the Greeks, the Romans, the Slaves, the Celts, and the Germans were living together within the same enclosures, nay, under the same roof. There was a time when out of many possible names for *father, mother, daughter, son, dog, cow, heaven,* and *earth*, those which we find in all the Aryan languages were framed, and obtained a mastery *in the struggle for life* which is carried on amongst synonymous words as much as among plants and animals.

Ibid, p.245.

Ethnology, the branch of anthropology concerned with race, provided a store of terms and ideas which Disraeli seized upon for an infinitely livelier novel than *Tancred, Lothair*. In Chapter 29 he introduced a Peacockian character called Mr Phoebus (Lord Leighton in real life), eminent painter upon 'Aryan principles' – 'not merely the study of nature, but of beautiful nature; the art of design in a country inhabited by a firstrate race, and where the laws, the manners, the customs, are calculated to maintain the health and beauty of a firstrate race.'

> Depend upon it, so strong and perfect a type as the original Aryan must be yet abundant among the millons, and may be developed. But for this you want great changes in your laws. It is the first duty of a state to attend to the frame and health of the subject. The Spartans understood this. They permitted no marriage the probable consequences of which might be a feeble progeny; they even took measures to secure a vigorous one. The Romans doomed the deformed to immediate destruction.

> Benjamin Disraeli, *Lothair* (1870), Chapter 29, 1881 edn, pp.136; 139.

In Chapter 76 Mr Phoebus holds out the faint possibility of positive improvement of the species, though his precise means are unclear.

> It would be something to sow the seeds of organic change in the Mongolian type, but I am not sanguine of success. There is no original fund of aptitude to act upon. The most ancient of existing communities is Turanian, and yet though they could invent gunpowder and the mariner's compass, they never could understand perspective.

> Ibid, Chapter 76, p.400.

Francis Galton had already made his preliminary suggestions concerning the possibility of improving the human race in two papers on 'Hereditary Talent and Character' in *Macmillan's Magazine* for 1865, though he did not coin 'eugenics' as a name for a new 'science' until his *Inquiries into Human Faculty and Development* (1883).

Mr Phoebus's insouciant embroidering of ideas is complemented by one of Disraeli's most comical inventions, an island near the Asian coast of the Aegean sea, which had 'an Aryan clime, an Aryan landscape, and an Aryan race'.

> 'I believe these islanders to be an unmixed race,' said Mr. Phoebus. 'The same form and visage prevails throughout; and very little has changed in anything, even in their religion.' . . .
> 'The Greek priests, particularly in these Asian islands, are good sort of people,' said Mr. Phoebus. 'They marry and have generally large families, often very beautiful. They have no sacerdotal feelings, for they never can have any preferment; all the high posts in the Greek Church being reserved for the monks, who study what is called theology. The Greek parish priest is not at all Semitic; there is nothing to counteract his Aryan tendencies. I have already raised the statue of a nymph at one of their favourite springs and places of pleasant pilgrimage, and I have a statue now in the island, still in its case, which I contemplate installing in a famous grove of laurel not far off and very much resorted to.'
>
> Ibid, Chapters 72-73, pp.385-87.

An even more elaborate use of ethnology, philology, and even craniology is apparent in Matthew Arnold's lectures on 'The Study of Celtic Literature' (*Cornhill Magazine*, March–July 1866). Celtic literature serves to bring together a number of fundamental Victorian concerns – origins, myths, the unity yet diversity of culture, the 'genius' or spirit of a people.

> What the French call the *science des origines*, the science of origins, – a science which is at the bottom of all real knowledge of the actual world, and which is every day growing in interest and importance, – is very incomplete without a thorough critical account of the Celts, and their genius, language and literature. . . .

Any one who knows the set of modern mythological science towards astronomical and solar myths, a set which has already justified itself in many respects so victoriously, and which is so irresistible that one can hardly now look up at the sun without having the sensations of a moth; that any one who knows this, should find in the Welsh remains no traces of mythology, is quite astounding. . . .

No doubt lands the most distant can be shown to have a common property in many marvellous stories. This is one of the most interesting discoveries of modern science; but modern science is equally interested in knowing how the genius of each people has differentiated, so to speak, this common property of theirs; in tracking out, in each case, that special 'variety of development', which, . . . 'the formative pressure of external circumstances' has occasioned; and not the formative pressure from without only, but also the formative pressure from within. . . .

Science has and will long have to be a divider and a separatist, breaking arbitrary and fanciful connections, and dissipating dreams of a premature and impossible unity. Still, science – true science – recognises in the bottom of her soul a law of ultimate fusion, of conciliation. To reach this, but to reach it legitimately, she tends. She draws, for instance, towards the same idea which fills her elder and diviner sister, poetry – the idea of the substantial unity of man; though she draws towards it by roads of her own. But continually she is showing us affinity where we imagined there was isolation. . . . The question is to be tried by external and by internal evidence; the language and the physical type of our race afford certain data for trying it, and the other data are afforded by our literature, genius, and spiritual production generally. Data of this second kind belong to the province of the literary critic; data of the first kind to the province of the philologist and of the physiologist.

Cornhill Magazine, Vol. 13, 1866, pp.287; 474; 477; 481; 539.

Arnold's analysis of 'the composite English genius', a term which had primary reference to a tutelary and controlling spirit, is now structured by contemporary ideas of affinity, gradation, speciation, hybridism and, above all, the hope of 'a new type, more intelligent, more gracious, and more humane' (Introduction) that we have already seen in Chambers and in Tennyson. Galton, Wells (*A Modern Utopia*, 1905) and others would hope to encourage the best existing types to produce more offspring. Mendel's theory of dominant and recessive traits, it should be mentioned, had been published obscurely at Brno in 1866 and was not brought to the attention of geneticists until 1900.

Evolutionary Anthropology

Arnold may have been helped in preparing his lectures by his friend, the Sanskrit scholar Max Müller. Müller had published an essay on comparative mythology in 1856 and this had led him to stress both the importance of 'the whole solar drama' and its priority.

> I consider that the very idea of divine powers sprang from the wonderment with which the forefathers of the Aryan family stared at the bright (deva) powers that came and went no one knew whence or whither, that never failed, never faded, never died, and were called immortal, i.e. unfading, as compared with the feeble and decaying race of man.
>
> F.M. Müller, *Lectures on the Science of Language* (1864), 1871 edn, Vol. 2, p.565.

The historical and comparative model of research provided by Sir William Jones, who in 1786 had suggested that the similarities between Sanskrit, Latin and Greek pointed to a common source, was very productive during the nineteenth century. But neither Arnold nor Müller was concerned with ape-like ancestors. 'Have brutes a soul?' Müller asked. 'Soul' he rejected immediately as a word so many times defined that 'it means everything and nothing'. But he kept 'brutes' and its implied premise, blankly shutting off the biological hypothesis that humans and certain higher animals might share a common ancestor.

> Where, then, is the difference between brute and man? What is it that man can do, and of which we find no signs, no rudiments, in the whole brute world? I answer without hesitation: the one great barrier between the brute and man is *Language*. Man speaks, and no brute has ever uttered a word. Language is our Rubicon, and no brute will dare cross it. This is our matter-of-fact answer to those who speak of development, who think they discover the rudiments at least of all human faculties in apes, and who would fain keep open the possibility that man is only a more favoured beast, the triumphant conqueror in the primeval struggle for life.
>
> Ibid, Vol. 1, pp.398; 402-403.

'We here saw the native Fuegian; an untamed savage is I really think', wrote Darwin to his sister on 30 March 1833, 'one of the most extraordinary spectacles in the world. – the difference between a domesticated & wild animal is far more strikingly marked in man. – in the naked barbarian, with his body coated with paint, whose very gestures, whether they may be peacible or hostile are unintelligible, with difficulty we see a fellow-creature' (*Correspondence* (1985), Vol. 1, pp.302-303). Man 'considered zoologically' is prominent in this sentence, and Darwin was to begin the *Origin of Species* with two chapters on 'Variation under Domestication' and 'Variation under Nature'. Could it have been their language that made Darwin recognise his common humanity? On 11 April, he wrote to J.S. Henslow, 'I shall never forget, when entering Good Success Bay, the yell with which a party received us. They were seated on a rocky point, surrounded by the dark forest of beech; as they threw their arms wildly round their heads & their long hair streaming they seemed the troubled spirits of another world' (Ibid, pp.306-307). Semiotically, they seem quite unsatisfactory! Neither language nor gestures communicate across bay or Rubicon. But Darwin was also using more traditional frames of reference. 'Untamed savage', 'barbarian' and 'troubled spirits of another world' seem classical in origin; Darwin's editors tell us that Captain Fitzroy of the *Beagle* thought of Caesar and the ancient Britons (like Conrad's Marlow). And though 'fellow-creature' was first used about 1648 to connect humans with plants and animals, one has little doubt that the Darwin who thought Carlyle's views about slavery were revolting had a more recent historical context in mind.

In maturity Darwin was sure that these men and women of Tierra del Fuego were immensely different from even the 'most highly organised' apes, which nevertheless he was proud to acknowledge for their heroism and compassion in a famous passage of the *Descent of Man and Selection in Relation to Sex* (Part 3, Chapter 21, Conclusion). But, crucially, all such intervals 'are connected by the finest gradations' and 'might pass and be developed into each other' (*Descent of Man* (1871), 1901 edn, pp.98-99). He contradicted Müller openly on the origin of articulate language. It arose out of instinctive cries, especially 'the musical tones and rhythm . . . used by our half-human ancestors, during the season of courtship' (pp.132; 871). E. Haeckel argued about this time for a kind of Monboddo-Peacock creature (pp.66-67 above), a primeval, but speechless, man who might have inhabited a lost continent now under the Indian Ocean. Haeckel's 'missing link' entered popular mythology. The 'season of courtship' proved irresistible to one of the subtlest novelists then writing.

'Science introduced us to our o'er-hoary ancestry – them in the Oriental posture', wrote Meredith in his Prelude to *The Egoist* (1879), 'whereupon we set up a primaeval chattering to rival the Amazon forest nigh nightfall'; but he continues, 'We have little to learn of apes, and they may be left.' Not entirely, however. Animal behaviour in general, such as the 'sexual selection' Darwin stressed so in the *Descent of Man*, to explain characteristics that seem more relevant to the struggle for mates than for survival – the brilliant tail-feathers of the peacock, 'the rank effluvium of the male goat' or the technicolour face of the adult male mandrill – can be used for the purposes of the Comic Spirit. Sir Willoughby Patterne is a

'model' Victorian hero, but he fits Darwin's description –
'Thus top-knots have appeared in several species' (*Descent of
Man* (1901), p.589).

> You spread a handsomer tail than your fellows; you
> dress a finer top-knot, you pipe a newer note, have a
> longer stride; she reviews you in competition, and
> selects you. . . . She cannot help herself; it is her nature,
> and her nature is the guarantee for the noblest race of
> men to come to her. In complimenting you, she is a
> promise of superior offspring. Science thus – or it is
> better to say, an acquaintance with science facilitates the
> cultivation of aristocracy. Consequently a successful
> pursuit and a wresting of her from a body of
> competitors, tell you that you are the best man. What is
> more, it tells the world so.
> Willoughby aired his amiable superlatives in the eye
> of Miss Middleton; he had a leg. He was the heir of
> successful competitors. He had a style, a tone, an artist
> tailor, an authority of manner: he had in the hopeful
> ardour of the chase among a multitude a freshness that
> gave him advantage; . . . .

> George Meredith, *The Egoist* (1879), Chapter 5,
> intro. V.S. Pritchett, 1972, pp.32-33.

For a time, the traditional issues of the social novel are seen in
Darwinian colours, but in Meredith's sophisticated fiction the
'purer' self is 'a person who more than ceases to be of use to us
after his ideal shall have led up men from their flint and
arrowhead caverns to inter-communicative daylight.'
Meredith was concerned with the subtler psychological
dangers of self-idealisation when the delusion of a 'purer' self
can first cause the individual 'to despise the mass, and then to
join the mass in crushing the individual' (*Diana of the
Crossways* (1884–85), Chapter 1).

Nevertheless, evolutionary biology pressed hard on both
anthropology and psychology in the last decades of the
nineteenth century, and consequently upon literature. Rider
Haggard's *She* (1886–87), Stevenson's *Dr. Jekyll and Mr. Hyde*

(1886) and those works of genius, the Mowgli stories by Kipling, are instances of writings that tread the boundaries between race and race, man and beast. In his 'theological grotesque', *The Island of Doctor Moreau*, H.G. Wells draws together in a kind of parable several threads – practical anatomy, physiology and all that relates to 'the plasticity of living forms'. Moreau's transformations are, in his eyes, no more than natural: 'The study of Nature makes a Man at last as remorseless as Nature' (p.116).

> 'But,' said I. 'These things – these animals *talk*!'
> He said that was so, and proceeded to point out that the possibilities of vivisection do not stop at a mere physical metamorphosis. A pig may be educated. The mental structure is even less determinate than the bodily. In our growing science of hypnotism we find the promise of a possibility of replacing old inherent instincts by new suggestions, grafting on or replacing the inherited fixed ideas. Very much, indeed, of what we call moral education is such an artificial modification and perversion of instinct; pugnacity is trained into courageous self-sacrifice, and suppressed sexuality into religious emotion. And the great difference between man and monkey is in the larynx, he said, in the incapacity to frame delicately different sound-symbols by which thought could be sustained.

> H.G. Wells, *The Island of Doctor Moreau* (1896),
> Chapter 14, p.112.

'In this', says the narrator, 'I failed to agree with him'. So too would Darwin, who quoted Müller's 1873 aphorism, 'There is no thought without words, as little as there are words without thought', and went on to exclaim, 'What a strange definition must here be given to the word thought! (*Descent of Man*, p.135n). But Darwin undoubtedly believed that 'the half-art, half-instinct of language still bears the stamp of its gradual evolution' and that 'the several mental and moral faculties of man have been gradually evolved'. He goes on to remark that 'we daily see these faculties developing in every infant' (Ibid, p.194). To *Mind* in 1877 he contributed 'A Biographical Sketch of an Infant', which ends, 'He understood one word, namely, his nurse's name, exactly before he invented his first word *mum*; and this is what might have been expected, as we know that the lower animals easily learn to understand spoken words' (Vol. 2, p.294). It is therefore not unexpected to find Moreau seizing upon the possibilities of transformation, mental as well as physical, inherent in the biology of the time. But the physical changes wrought by surgery would never be transmitted to the next generation, and in the context of the fable Moreau forgets that transformation also includes reversion.

> He who rejects with scorn the belief that the shape of his own canines, and their occasional great development in other men, are due to our early forefathers having been provided with these formidable weapons, will probably reveal, by sneering, the line of his descent. For though he no longer intends, nor has the power, to use these teeth as weapons, he will unconsciously retract his 'snarling muscles' . . . so as to expose them ready for action, like a dog prepared to fight.
>
> Charles Darwin, *The Descent of Man* (1871), 1901 edn, pp.60-61.

Mythology

Charles Lyell once quipped that as far as the descent of man was concerned, he couldn't go the whole orang! Alfred Wallace was another major dissentient. Natural selection might have worked on 'a single homogeneous race without the faculty of speech, and probably inhabiting some tropical region'; it might even have accounted for the differences between the various races of humankind as they spread out over the surface of the earth. But as soon as human beings began to take thought, to make spears and plant seeds, they transcended the laws of natural selection (Greene, *The Death of Adam*, pp.316-19). He gave his views still wider circulation in the *Quarterly Review* for 1869. The 'faculty of abstraction', as Müller put it, the ability to represent symbolically, seemed absolute proof to many that humans differed in kind from animals. The realisation of this was in itself a mark of human progress.

> The sense of an absolute psychical distinction between man and beast, so prevalent in the civilized world, is hardly to be found among the lower races. Men to whom the cries of beasts and birds seem like human language, and their actions guided as it were by human thought, logically enough allow the existence of souls to beasts, birds, and reptiles, as to men. The lower psychology cannot but recognize in beasts the very characteristics which it attributes to the human soul, namely, the phenomena of life and death, will and judgment, and the phantom seen in vision or in dream. . . .
> Although, however, the primitive belief in the souls of animals still survives to some extent in serious philosophy, it is obvious that the tendency of educated opinion on the question whether brutes have soul, as distinguished from life and mind, has for ages been in a negative and sceptical direction. The doctrine has fallen from its once high estate. It belonged originally to real, though rude science.

> E.B. Tylor, *Primitive Culture: Researches into the Development of Mythology, Philosophy, Religion, Language, Art, and Custom* (1871), 1873 edn, Vol. 1, pp.469; 471.

Tylor was a distinguished anthropologist. Using ethnographic, archeological and other forms of evidence, he discussed with complete lucidity a great range of instances and, for him, phases of human culture. He assumed a universal pattern of development, but moving at different rates of progress: 'To the human intellect in its early childlike state may be assigned the origin and first development of myth. . . . we may . . . claim the savage as a representative of the childhood of the human race' (Ibid, Vol. 1, p.284). His use of phrases like 'the lower psychology', 'the lower tribes' or 'the primitive belief' implies developmental continuity with 'the civilized world'. It can even be accompanied with a sense of loss when his sympathetic relativism struggles with his rationality.

> Wanting the power of transporting himself into this imaginative atmosphere, the student occupied with the analysis of the mythic world may fail so pitiably in conceiving its depth and intensity of meaning, as to convert it into stupid fiction. Those can see more justly who have the poet's gift of throwing their minds back into the world's older life, like the actor who for a moment can forget himself and become what he pretends to be. Wordsworth, that 'modern ancient' as Max Müller has so well called him, could write of Storm and Winter, or of the naked Sun climbing the sky, as though he were some Vedic poet at the head-spring of the Aryan race, 'seeing' with his mind's eye a mythic hymn to Agni or Varuna.

> Ibid, Vol. 1, p.305.

Tylor is as aware as any Victorian Romantic of the torpedo touch of the modern age that numbed creativity and paralysed the sympathetic imagination: 'the civilized European may contrast his own stiff orderly prosaic thought with the wild shifting poetry and legend of the old myth-maker' (p.305). Or read Matthew Arnold's poem 'The Scholar Gypsy', we might add.

A flourishing Victorian genre of fantasy literature – the nonsense verse of Lear and Carroll, the fairy comedies of W.S. Gilbert, the Celtic stories of 'Fiona Macleod' (William Sharp) – proves that the modern European had not lost the power of invention. We might even be transported to the thought world of nineteenth-century anthropology, as in *'That Very Mab'*, published anonymously by May Kendall and Andrew Lang. Shakespeare's fairy comes to contemporary England, where she is captured by a professor, who thinks she is a new kind of butterfly and pops her in a glass bottle. There she becomes the heart of a child's game.

'You never saw anybody play at that kind of game before?'

'No,' said the child, 'nobody ever.'

'Then,' cried the professor, in a loud and blissful voice, 'we have at last discovered the origin of religion. It isn't Ghosts. It isn't the Infinite. It is worshipping butterflies, with a service of fetich stones. The boy has returned to it by an act of unconscious inherited memory, derived from Palaeolithic Man, who must, therefore, have been the native of a temperate climate, where there were green lepidoptera. O my friends, what a thing is inherited memory! In each of us there slumber all the impressions of all our predecessors, up to the earliest Ascidian [minute marine creature]. See how the domesticated dog,' cried the professor, forgetting that he was not lecturing in Albemarle Street, 'see how the domesticated dog, by inherited memory, turns round on the hearthrug before he curls up in sleep! He is unconsciously remembering the long grasses in which his wild ancestors dwelt. Also observe this boy, who has retained an unconscious recollection of the earliest creed of prehistoric man.

M. Kendall and A. Lang, *'That Very Mab'* (1885),
Chapter 3, pp.40-41.

The targets are several: Müller defined the Infinite as that which is perceived by Faith (*Lectures on the Science of Language*, Vol. 2, p.632); Tylor treated Fetishism, 'the doctrine of spirits' connected with certain material objects, as a branch of Animism, the belief in spiritual beings (*Primitive Culture*, Vol. 2, p.144); Darwin and lecturers at the Royal Institution are also glanced at. Nor do the arts escape, as a Wilde-like poet speaks.

'I am a poet,' said the poet. 'I bow to no narrow machinery of definitions. Words have a gemlike beauty and colour of their own. They are *not* merely the signs of ideas – of thoughts.'

'I wish they were!' groaned the professor. 'They are with us.'

'The idea,' continued the poet, 'must conform to the word, when the word honours the idea by making use of it. What care I for the conventional, the threadbare significance? My heart recognises, through the outer garment of apparent insanity, the inner adaptability. Soar, my mind!' . . .

Those readers who have not yet perused the poet's sonnet may recognise it, of course, by the first line:
'Fair denizen of deathless ether, doomed.'
It attracted a good deal of attention at the time. . . .

The professor also sent to the 'Spectator' an account of the Origin of Religion, as developed by his little boy, under his very eyes. But the editor thought, not unnaturally, that it was only the professor's fun, and declined to publish it, preferring an essay on the Political Rights of the Domesticated Cat.

M. Kendall and A. Lang, *'That Very Mab'* (1885),
Chapter 4, pp.54-55; 58-60.

In this swift-moving little satire Kendall and Lang encompass the purely biological (seeing bishops as 'an unnecessary organ, merely transmitted by inheritance in the national organism'), the social ('colonisation of the lunar world by emigration of the able-bodied unemployed'), the political ('Dynamite, that last infirmity of noble minds, should only be resorted to when all other modes of conciliation have failed'), as well as the anthropological and the aesthetic.

Mythography, Ancient and Modern

Tylor's *Primitive Culture* is a remarkable compendium of myths.

The Zulus still tell the tale of an Amafeme tribe who became baboons. They were an idle race who did not like to dig, but wished to eat at other people's houses, ... They fastened on behind them the handles of their now useless digging picks, these grew and became tails, hair made its appearance on their bodies, their foreheads became overhanging, and so they became baboons, ... Mr. Kingsley's story of the great and famous nation of the Doasyoulikes, who degenerated by natural selection into gorillas, is the civilized counterpart of this savage myth. . . . The myths of human degeneration and development have much more in common with the speculations of Lord Monboddo than with the anatomical arguments of Professor Huxley.

E.B. Tylor, *Primitive Culture* (1871), Vol. 1, pp.376-77; 379.

The certainty of Huxley's physical anthropology depends upon measurement and rational analysis of physical phenomena. The same kind of validity cannot be attained by Tylor's anthropology, his comparative analysis of human culture. But 'Myths of relation of Apes to Men by development or degeneration', products of 'real, though rude science', now include all scientific explanations of his day that have been superseded. As he himself wrote, 'Progress, degradation, survival, revival, modification, are all modes of the connexion that binds together the complex network of civilization' (Ibid, Vol. 1, p.17). There is too the question of the nature of our belief in myths. Stories of vampires may, as Tylor suggests, have once been serious explanations of wasting diseases. Bram Stoker knew that there would be a readership for *Dracula* in 1897. We must admit that tales of vampires, werewolves, spirit-possession and planets of the apes fill our books and screens, popularity assured and disbelief still suspended.

Tylor himself demonstrated the curious entanglements of story and history, fact and legend, name and nonsense, myth and metaphor. He wrote of religion too and its connections with ritual, in part 'expressive and symbolic performances, the dramatic utterance of religious thought, the gesture-language of theology', in part 'means of intercourse with and influence on spiritual beings' (Ibid, Vol. 2, p.362). Tylor and J.G. Frazer might assert the triumph of rational progress, but their evidence went to augment a powerful counter-movement already in operation. Müller thought mythology 'a disease of language', names or metaphors foolishly taken literally. He was particularly incensed with a pseudo-religious use of the word 'Nothing', asserting that language 'has reached to an almost delirious state, and ceased to be what it was meant to be, the expression of the impressions felt through the senses, or the conceptions of a rational mind' (Vol. 2, p.381). But the opposition is too pat. Its scientism (*OED*, 1877) may even be a major cause of the opposite path taken by the great writers of the turn of the century – Yeats, Conrad, Joyce and Eliot, revivers of the mythological.

Müller's contempt for Nirvana is effectively answered by Conrad's Marlow, in his 'pose of a Buddha preaching in European clothes', telling of the changes that had taken place in his cranium, which had been scientifically measured with calipers by a company doctor at the outset of his quest 'back to the earliest beginnings of the world' in Africa ('The Heart of Darkness', *Blackwood's Magazine*, Vol. 165, 1899, pp.196; 201; 481). Though Conrad's narrator declared that 'we live, as we dream – alone', he struggled like De Quincey or Coleridge to 'convey the dream-sensation, that commingling of absurdity, surprise, and bewilderment' of his experiences, using a language that might be 'the pulsating stream of light, or the deceitful flow from the heart of an impenetrable darkness' (Ibid, pp.216-17; 495). The opposition may seem as pat, but it is now intended to convey the range of ambiguities possible, just as Marlow's account of colonial exploitation in the Congo is an attempt to explore the anthropological and psychological enigmas of human habits and beliefs. Ultimately, Conrad probably thought with Marlow, life is inexplicable, but he was prepared to test to the utmost the suggestive powers of words and imagery. The company doctor's measurements are farcically irrelevant.

Conrad's narrative stance in *Heart of Darkness* has what Cedric Watts has called 'a recessive adroitness', but the famous comparative method of nineteenth-century anthropology is very evident in Part 1. Contemporary colonial ventures are given a context of British savagery two thousand years before, when Roman triremes sailed up a Thames at the end of the known world. In Africa Conrad evokes 'primeval' mud and forest, recalls a bizarre speculation that on Mars people went about on all-fours (p.216) and rivals Milton or Darwin in his natural description.

> The great wall of vegetation, an exuberant and entangled mass of trunks, branches, leaves, boughs, festoons, motionless in the moonlight, was like a rioting invasion of soundless life, a rolling wave of plants, piled up, crested, ready to topple over the creek, to sweep every little man of us out of his little existence. And it moved not. A deadened burst of mighty splashes and snorts reached us from afar, as though an ichthyosaurus had been taking a bath of glitter in the great river.

Joseph Conrad, 'The Heart of Darkness', Part 1, p.219.

This palaeontological depth continues in Part 2 with allusions to a prehistoric earth on which wandered the first of men; the parallels with contemporary cannibals are definitely established: 'They still belonged to the beginnings of time – had no inherited experience to teach them as it were' (p.488). All leads up to the presentation of Kurtz, European 'emissary of pity, and science, and progress, and devil knows what else' (p.214), a voice that proclaimed idealism and extermination, a lofty frontal bone that shone like the ivory sought with such imbecile rapacity.

> All Europe contributed to the making of Kurtz; and by-and-by I learned that, most appropriately, the International Society for the Suppression of Savage Customs had intrusted him with the making of a report, for their future guidance. And he had written it too. I've seen it. I've read it. It was eloquent, vibrating with eloquence, but too high-strung, I think. Seventeen pages of close writing he had found time for! But this must have been before his – let us say – nerves went wrong, and caused him to preside at certain midnight dances ending with unspeakable rites, which – as far as I reluctantly gathered from what I heard at various times – were offered up to him – do you understand? – to Mr

Kurtz himself. But it was a beautiful piece of writing. The opening paragraph, however, in the light of later information, strikes me now as ominous. He begins with the argument that we whites, from the point of development we had arrived at 'must necessarily appear to them [savages] in the nature of supernatural beings – we approach them with the might as of deity,' and so on, and so on.

Joseph Conrad 'The Heart of Darkness', Part 2,
pp.497-98.

In Part 1 Marlow told his companions that 'the conquest of the earth, which mostly means the taking it away from those who have a different complexion or slightly flatter noses than ourselves' is only redeemed by 'an unselfish belief in the idea – something you can set up, and bow down before, and offer a sacrifice to' (p.196). Kurtz had managed to incarnate the idea of empire in himself, but in Part 3 an atavistically degenerate Kurtz is found crawling in the wilderness that had awakened his 'forgotten and brutal instincts' (pp.644-45) – crawling 'on all-fours', Conrad added in a later edition. It is impossible to draw together all the threads of this complex modern masterpiece; the recapitulatory structure of *Heart of Darkness* can itself be seen as a consequence of the layered, web-like understanding of human existence achieved by the life sciences in the nineteenth century. But it would be wrong to omit the paradoxical loyalty Marlow gave to Kurtz and his refusal 'to affirm the fellow was exactly worth the life we lost in getting to him', that of his savage helmsman, killed by a spear from the jungle.

He steered for me – I had to look after him, I worried about his deficiencies, and thus a subtle bond had been created, of which I only became aware when it was suddenly broken. And the intimate profundity of that look he gave me when he received his hurt remains to this day in my memory – like a claim of distant kinship affirmed in a supreme moment.

Ibid, Part 2, pp.498-99.

5 Science and Literature

Early Nineteenth Century

In *Science in Culture: The Early Victorian Period* S.F. Cannon illustrates 'the fundamental difference in the role of science between early Victorian times and our own day': science as norm of truth rather than science as power or science as progressive knowledge, as it is for us. The key science then was physical astronomy, its avatar Newton. William Blake was as unorthodox in this respect as in everything else.

> Your religion, O deists, 'Deism', is the worship of the god of this world by the means of what you call Natural Religion and Natural Philosophy, and of natural morality or self-righteousness, the selfish virtues of the natural heart.

>   *   *   *

> But the spectre like a hoar-frost & a mildew rose over Albion
> Saying: 'I am God, O sons of men! I am your rational power!
> Am I not Bacon & Newton & Locke who teach humility to man,
> Who teach doubt & experiment? And my two wings, Voltaire, Rousseau?'

>   *   *   *

> Then Albion drew England into his bosom in groans & tears;
> But she stretched out her starry night in spaces against him, like
> A long serpent, in the abyss of the spectre; which augmented

The night with dragon wings covered with stars; & in
the wings
Jerusalem & Vala appeared; & above, between the
wings magnificent
The Divine Vision dimly appeared in clouds of blood,
weeping.

> William Blake, *Jerusalem* (1804–c.20), Chapter 3
> and Preface, in *Poems* (1971), pp.732-33; 737-38.

Wordsworth's view was more variable. In a passage added to
the 1800 Preface to the second edition of *Lyrical Ballads*, the
first edition of which had been seen through the press by Davy,
he drew some very deliberate distinctions.

The knowledge both of the Poet and the Man of Science
is pleasure; but the knowledge of the one cleaves to us as
a necessary part of our existence, our natural and
unalienable inheritance; the other is a personal and
individual acquisition, slow to come to us, and by no
habitual and direct sympathy connecting us with our
fellow-beings. The Man of Science seeks truth as a
remote and unknown benefactor; he cherishes it and
loves it in his solitude; the Poet, singing a song in which
all human beings join with him, rejoices in the presence
of truth as our visible friend and hourly companion.
Poetry is the breath and finer spirit of all knowledge;
it is the impassioned expression which is in the
countenance of all Science. . . . Poetry is the first and
last of all knowledge – it is as immortal as the heart of
man. If the labours of men of science should ever create
any material revolution, direct or indirect, in our
condition, and in the impressions which we habitually
receive, the Poet will sleep no more than at present, but
he will be ready to follow the steps of the man of
Science, not only in those general indirect effects, but he
will be at his side, carrying sensation into the midst
of the objects of the Science itself. The remotest
discoveries of the Chemist, the Botanist, or
Mineralogist, will be as proper objects of the Poet's art

as any upon which it can be employed, if the time should ever come when these things shall be familiar to us, and the relations under which they are contemplated by the followers of these respective Sciences shall be manifestly palpable and material to us as enjoying and suffering beings. If the time should ever come when what is now called Science, thus familiarized to men, shall be ready to put on, as it were, a form of flesh and blood, the Poet will lend his divine spirit to aid the transfiguration, and will welcome the Being thus produced, as a dear and genuine inmate of the household of man.

> W. Wordsworth and S.T. Coleridge, *Lyrical Ballads* (1798), ed. W.J.B. Owen, Oxford, 2nd edn 1969, p.168.

If Wordsworth did not see the scientist as bearer of the fullness of truth, he at least came to see him as on a voyage of discovery.

And from my pillow, looking forth by light
Of moon or favouring stars, I could behold
The antechapel where the statue stood
Of Newton with his prism and silent face,
The marble index of a mind for ever
Voyaging through strange seas of Thought, alone.

> William Wordsworth, *The Prelude* (1850) Book 3, ll.58-63.

The last two lines were added about 1838.

Herschel gave precision to the search and related it to literature, if only by loose analogy.

We must never forget that it is principles, not phenomena, – laws, not insulated independent facts, – which are the objects of enquiry to the natural philosopher. As truth is single, and consistent with itself, a principle may be as completely and as plainly elucidated by the most familiar and simple fact, as by the most imposing and uncommon phenomenon. The colours which glitter on a soap-bubble are the immediate consequence of a principle the most important from the variety of phenomena it explains, and the most beautiful, from its simplicity and compendious neatness, in the whole science of optics. . . .

And this is, in fact, one of the great sources of delight which the study of natural science imparts to its votaries. A mind which has once imbibed a taste for scientific enquiry, and has learnt the habit of applying its principles readily to the cases which occur, has within itself an inexhaustible source of pure and exciting contemplations: – one would think that Shakespeare had such a mind in view when he describes a contemplative man as finding

"Tongues in trees – books in the running brooks – Sermons in stones – and good in every thing."

John Herschel, *Preliminary Discourse* (1831), 1832 edn, pp.13-15.

It is easy to vulgarise this insight, both in attack and defence. G.H. Lewes delivered a comic onslaught on those who moralised fairy tales, called stories a waste of time and taught sciences 'adapted to the infant mind'.

Most wise doctors! Most credulous parents! Most unhappy children! To you all, a blessed millenium of science is coming, wherein imagination and emotion will no more vitiate the mind; wherein 'prejudices' will be matters of research, and the differential calculus be expounded to the infant in the cradle! – A time when 'gentle maidens reading through their tears' will feel their hearts tremble over – conic sections; romantic youths will feel their breasts inflated with the mystery and magic of – the composition of forces; and happy men have all their sympathies enlarged by eccentric orbits! Then will the air be filled with sighs of 'definite proportions;' and the dance – theatre – and pic-nic, give place to scientific meetings. Then will the budding rose of womanhood meet her chosen one, beneath the

> mystic moon, and pour forth her feelings on the atomic theory: her lover answering in impassioned descriptions of stalactite and strata!

G.H. Lewes, Ranthorpe (1847), pp.192-93.

The irony merely reinforces the simple separation of science and literature, and Herschel's contemplative man can only retire with lowered eyes when such rhetorical jumping jacks are lit. Darwin reports that Herschel, who was internationally regarded as *the* representative British scientist, was very shy and 'often had a distressed expression', always coming into a room, according to a friend who admired his qualities too, 'as if he knew that his hands were dirty, and that he knew that his wife knew that they were dirty' (*Autobiographies*, p.63). Nevertheless, science and literature were associated in one very important respect in the first half of the nineteenth century. What Cannon calls the 'fallacy of substituting logical classification for direct knowledge' (p.21) is rejected in famous literary instances – Wordsworth's poem 'The Tables Turned' (1798) and Dickens' *Hard Times* (1854) – and in the writings of first-class scientists. Cannon cites unfamiliar but apposite passages.

> Let us suppose that a zoologist should attempt to give an account of some animal, a porcupine for instance, to people who had never seen it. The porcupine, he might say, is of the genus mammalia, and the order glires. There are whiskers on its face; it is two feet long; it has four toes before, five behind, two fore teeth, and eight grinders. Its body is covered with hair and quills. And, when all this has been said, would any one of the auditors have formed a just idea of a porcupine?

T.B. Macaulay, 'John Dryden' (1828); Works
(1898), Vol. 7, p.119.

Whewell's acute analytical mind came to the same conclusion.

> It is a curious example of the influence of the belief in definitions, that elementary books have been written in which Natural History is taught in the way of question

and answer, and consequently by means of words alone. In such a scheme, of course all objects are *defined*: and we may easily anticipate the value of the knowledge thus conveyed. Thus, 'Iron is a well-known hard metal, of a darkish gray colour, and very elastic.' 'Copper is an orange-coloured metal, more sonorous than any other, and the most elastic of any except iron.' This is to pervert the meaning of education, and to make it a business of mere words.

William Whewell, *Philosophy* (1840), Vol. 2, pp.519-20.

Moreover, the most recent research is beginning to stress that both scientists and creative writers were then united in a very special way; they 'belonged in the same company as those who put forth the new philology, with its insistence on the exercise of a full imaginative consciousness in the investigation of the life of the past' (R. Preyer, 'The Romantic Tide Reaches Trinity', in *Victorian Science and Victorian Values: Literary Perspectives*, eds J. Paradis and T. Postlethwaite (1981), pp.52; 56).

Now a language will often be wiser, not merely than the vulgar, but even than the wisest of those who speak it. Being like amber in its efficacy to circulate the electric spirit of truth, it is also like amber in embalming and preserving the relics of ancient wisdom, although one is not seldom puzzled to decipher its contents. Sometimes it locks up truths, which were once well known, but which in the course of ages have passed out of sight and been forgotten. In other cases it holds the germs of truths, of which, though they were never plainly discerned, the genius of the framers caught a glimpse in a happy moment of divination.

J. and A. Hare, *Guesses at Truth by Two Brothers* (1827), Boston 1865, pp.234-35.

Such statements were made at a time when a fuller analytical understanding of the relation between principles and phenomena was increasingly informed by the realisation of what might be learnt from past development – of languages and cultures, rock strata and fossil remains, biota and environments. They look forward to the developments we have seen in Chapters 3 and 4 above.

Later Nineteenth Century

In 1872 Matthew Arnold published *A Bible-Reading for Schools*. Its introduction contains relatively unguarded but significant passages that were later omitted when an edition was prepared for more general use.

> The advantage to any branch of study of possessing good and compendious text-books it is impossible to overrate. The several natural sciences, too, from their limited and definite character, admit better of being advantageously presented by short text-books than such a wide and indefinite subject-matter, – nothing less than the whole history of the human spirit, – as that which belongs to letters; and this inherent advantage men of skill and talent, like the authors of the text-books I speak of, are just the people to turn to the best account. . . .
>
> An ounce of practice, they say, is better than a pound of theory; and certainly one may talk for ever about the wonder-working power of letters, and yet produce no good at all, unless one really puts people in the way of feeling this power. The friends of physics do not content themselves with extolling physics; they put forth school-books by which the study of physics may be with proper advantage brought near to those who before were strangers to it; and they do wisely. For any one who believes in the civilising power of letters and often talks of this belief, to think that he has for more than twenty years got his living by inspecting schools for the people, has gone in and out among them, has seen that the power of letters never reaches them at all and that the whole study of letters is thereby discredited

and its power called in question, and yet has attempted nothing to remedy this state of things, can not but be vexing and disquieting. ... he may well desire to do something to pay his debt to popular education before he finally departs, ...

> Matthew Arnold, *A Bible-Reading for Schools*, in *Complete Prose Works*, ed. R.H. Super, Vol. 7 (1970), pp.500; 505.

It is very inadequate to speak of the 'limited and definite character' of science in an age when, for example, John Tyndall kept recurring to the absolute need for a ranging, boldly speculative imagination in scientific research, fully Romantic in its dissatisfaction with the constraints imposed by the sensible material world in which we live. There is no sense of a competitive relationship in this respect but Arnold, who was an agile, ironical and effective publicist, was to refine his view in 'Literature and Science', which probably voiced the majority opinion of literate people.

Arnold's occasion was an address by his friend, and polemical rival, T.H. Huxley, made at the opening of a Science College in Birmingham where 'mere literary instruction and education' were to be prohibited. Arnold's lecture was delivered to a crowded audience in the Cambridge Senate House, published in the *Nineteenth Century* for August 1882, and then delivered again and again in a lecture tour of America. There is no doubt that he felt himself to be answering the chief Victorian spokesman for science, giving what R.H. Super regards as 'the epitome, the almost perfect statement of his doctrine' (*Complete Prose Works*, Vol. 10, 1974, pp.462-64) on behalf of literature.

> Let us, I say, be agreed about the meaning of the terms we are using. I talk of knowing the best which has been thought and uttered in the world; Professor Huxley says this means knowing *literature*. Literature is a large word; it may mean everything written with letters or printed in a book. Euclid's *Elements* and Newton's *Principia* are thus literature. All knowledge

that reaches us through books is literature. But by literature Professor Huxley means *belles lettres*. He means to make me say, that knowing the best which has been thought and said by the modern nations is knowing their *belles lettres* and no more. And this is no sufficient equipment, he argues, for a criticism of modern life. But as I do not mean, by knowing ancient Rome, knowing merely more or less of Latin *belles lettres*, and taking no account of Rome's military and political and legal and administrative work in the world; and as, by knowing ancient Greece, I understand knowing her as the giver of Greek art, and the guide to a free and right use of reason and to scientific method, and the founder of our mathematics and physics and astronomy and biology – I understand knowing her as all this, and not merely knowing certain Greek poems, histories, and speeches – so as to the knowledge of modern nations also. By knowing modern nations, I mean not merely knowing their *belles lettres*, but knowing also what has been done by such men as Copernicus, Galileo, Newton, Darwin. . . .

Interesting, indeed, these results of science are, important they are, and we should all be acquainted with them. But what I now wish you to mark is, that we are still, when they are propounded to us and we receive them, we are still in the sphere of intellect and knowledge. And for the generality of men there will be found, I say, to arise, when they have duly taken in the proposition that their ancestor was 'a hairy quadruped furnished with a tail and pointed ears, probably arboreal in his habits', there will be found to arise an invincible desire to relate this proposition to the sense within them for conduct and to the sense for beauty. But this the men of science will not do for us, and will hardly, even, profess to do. They will give us other pieces of knowledge, other facts, about other animals and their ancestors, or about plants, or about stones, or about stars; and they may finally bring us to those 'general conceptions of the universe which have been forced upon us,' says Professor Huxley, 'by physical science.' But still it will be knowledge only which they give us; knowledge not put for us into relation with our sense for conduct, our sense for beauty, and touched with emotion by being so put; not thus put for us, and therefore, to the majority of mankind, after a certain while unsatisfying, wearying. . . .

I have heard it said that the sagacious and admirable naturalist whom we have lately lost, Mr. Darwin, once owned to a friend that for his part he did not experience the necessity for two things which most men find so necessary to them – poetry and religion; science and the domestic affections, he thought, were enough. . . . But then Darwins are very rare. Another great and admirable master of natural knowledge, Faraday, was a Sandemanian. That is to say, he related his knowledge to his instinct for conduct and to his instinct for beauty by the aid of that respectable Scottish sectary, Robert Sandeman. And for one man among us with the disposition to do as Darwin did in this respect, there are fifty, probably, with the disposition to do as Faraday.

Matthew Arnold, 'Literature and Science',
Nineteenth Century, Vol. 12, 1882, pp.220–21;
224–25.

There is some validity in these propositions but a snippet from Darwin's *Descent of Man* (1871) is an extraordinary reduction of this work's value for psychology and anthropology (sciences ignored altogether in the lecture) and Darwin's loss in later years of 'the higher aesthetic tastes' is no argument against the intense delight he found in poetry, Shakespeare and music during the first part of his life (*Autobiographies*, p.83). One might even note the models of affective decline in Wordsworth's 'Immortality Ode' (1807) and Coleridge's 'Dejection' (1802). The keenest critique of all Victorian orotundity, however, both scientific and literary, came in the brilliant parodies by a young contemporary of the embattled cultural mammoths. In *The New Republic: Culture, Faith and Philosophy in an English Country House* W.H.

Mallock makes one of his scientists orate like Gladstone, who made Queen Victoria feel like a public meeting when he addressed her.

'Is not science essentially religious, essentially poetical – nay, does it not deepen quite boundlessly the religion and poetry already existing in the world, and fuse the two together, as they were never fused before? Does it narrow our notions of life's wonder and dignity to peer into the abyss of being, and learn something of the marvellous laws of things – to discover the same mysterious Something in a snowflake, in the scent of a rose, in the 'topmost star of unascended heaven,' and in some prayer or aspiration in the soul of Man? True it is that this wondrous All is Matter, and that all matter is atoms in its last analysis. . . .

Let us agree about conduct – morality, by-the-by, is the plainer word – that is the great thing. Let us agree about the noble and the beautiful. Let us agree heroically to follow truth – ay, truth; let us follow that, I say, picking our way step by step, and not look where we are going. Let us follow – what can I add to this? – the incomparable life of the great Founder of Christianity. Yes, Miss Merton, entertaining the views that I do, I say the incomparable life. Such is the message of science to the world; such is the instinct of culture when enriched and quickened by science.'

This was literally taking the bread out of Mr. Luke's mouth. Not only was it repeating what he had said before, but it was anticipating, in a formless undisciplined way, the very thing that he was going to say again. And the man who had robbed him thus was a mere Philistine – a mere man of science, who was without even a smattering of Greek or Hebrew, and who thought sensori-motor nerves and spontaneous generation more important subjects than Marcion's Gospel or the Psalms of David. For once in his life Mr. Luke was for the moment completely silenced.

W.H. Mallock, *The New Republic* (1877), Book 3, Chapter 3 (1975), pp.219-20; 225-26.

Mallock has caught more than the topics and asseverations of Tyndall (Stockton) and Arnold (Luke), he has moved into the exalted atmosphere in which they both had their public being. There was too much of what Miss Merton (Mallock's cousin in real life) called 'moral ozone in the air'. Without reverting to the kind of obsessive concern with concrete knowledge displayed by men like Josiah Wedgwood in the early part of the century, it was time to come closer to common life.

> When the shadows shortened and the lama leaned more heavily on Kim, there was always the Wheel of Life to draw forth, to hold flat under wiped stones, and with a long straw to expound cycle by cycle. Here sat the Gods on high – and they were dreams of dreams. Here was our Heaven and the world of the demi-Gods – horsemen fighting among the hills. Here were the agonies done upon the beasts, souls ascending or descending the ladder and therefore not to be interfered with. Here were the Hells, hot and cold, and the abodes of tormented ghosts. Let the *chela* [disciple] study the troubles that came from over-eating – bloated stomach and burning bowels. Obediently then, with bowed head and brown finger alert to follow the pointer, did the *chela* study; but when they came to the Human World, busy and profitless, that is just above the Hells, his mind was distracted; for by the roadside trundled the very Wheel itself, eating, drinking, trading, marrying, and quarrelling – all warmly alive.

> Rudyard Kipling, *Kim* (1901), Chapter 12, 1902 edn, p.302.

A Modern Critical Approach

Tennyson's early work 'The Devil and the Lady' is remarkable, but it displays no more than an incidental selection of scientific items from the countless number available. Gliserman's analysis of his mature responses to the larger movements of scientific thought in his time takes us well beyond the kind of literary assessment that takes scientific ideas and data as given, if not exactly for granted. She reads the texts by which science was disseminated as we are accustomed to read more obviously 'creative' works, because they too revise reality and affect attitudes, by means which are often indistinguishable. Gillian Beer's distinguished study marks a strengthening of this line of approach to the integrated discourses of science and of literature. The first major section of her book is devoted to the context, development, longings and recognitions of Darwin's own imagination; to his struggles with the blocking assumptions and beliefs of his culture, particularly as they are embodied in language and language use, and to his powerful revisions of existing myths and narrative sequences. She sees evolutionary theory itself as 'a form of imaginative history'. It could not be proved by simple experiment, but insofar as its arguments were conveyed through multiple instances and declared relationships, it emphasised cause and effect, descent and kin, and – in Darwin – an 'eschewing of fore-ordained design', since selection operated upon variations that had appeared in a random manner with respect to their future history (Gillian Beer, *Darwin's Plots*, p.8).

A single but significant example may be taken from the *Origin of Species*. In the first edition of 1859 Darwin wrote, 'It may be said that natural selection is daily and hourly scrutinising, throughout the world, every variation, even the slightest; rejecting that which is bad, preserving and adding up all that is good; . . .' (Chapter 4). He meant that when, somehow, plants or animals that did not exactly resemble their parent stock appeared, they would survive if they were adapted to the natural conditions they met in life and could transmit their characteristics to their own offspring. Such an apparently blind and random process is not easily associated with a concept of purpose but Darwin has slipped into a turn of phrase that makes him appear to believe in an intelligent designer, 'who does nothing in vain, who acts by the shortest mode, who does all for the best', as St Hilaire put it (p.17 above). If we consult Morse Peckham's Variorum Text of the *Origin of Species*, which prints all the changes found in the first six editions, we find that Darwin has revised this sentence to begin, 'It may metaphorically be said . . . .' (p.169)! In subsequent editions he made further exasperated efforts to deny the intentionalist bias which God or man-centred systems of thought seem to force upon the expression of this key topic: 'In the literal sense of the word, no doubt, natural selection is a misnomer; but who ever objected to chemists speaking of the elective affinities of the various elements? . . .'; 'It has been said that I speak of natural selection as an active power or Deity; but who objects to an author speaking of the attraction of gravity as ruling the movements of the planets?' (p.165). Reasonable questions – but Darwin, a great reader of literature, might in reply have been asked to consider the ways in which Pope had exploited the ambiguities of language in *The Dunciad* (1743), where dunces experience no difficulty in finding their mother-goddess, Dullness: 'None need a guide, by sure Attraction led, / And strong impulsive gravity of Head' (Book 4, ll.75-76). The word 'gravity' comes from the Latin *gravitas*, 'weight', and was first introduced in a favourable figurative sense, associated with wisdom. Seventeenth-century scientists, however, chose to employ it in a physical sense close to the Latin root-meaning. And then Pope relit a dark torch of metaphor. (See *OED*, and D. Davie, *The Language of Science and the Language of Literature, 1700–1740* (1963), p.30.) It is not easy to control language in action. In Darwin's original sentence several traps were sprung: selection implies the existence of a selector; selection functions grammatically as an agent; any truly new formulation of ideas on this topic such as Darwin's must make way against a strongly-flowing tide of assumption that successful life-forms (especially human) surely had an intelligent cause. Adaptation and design (often 'Design') combined only too easily with each other, manifested an elective affinity, so to speak.

Before proceeding to her penetrating criticism of nineteenth-century fiction Gillian Beer demonstrates the range and significance of cultural exchange in Darwin's main writings – the profound influence of Milton and, more broadly, the imaginative patterns and sequences he shared with his literate contemporaries, readers as well as writers:

Darwinian theory takes up elements from older orders and particularly from recurrent mythic themes such as transformation and metamorphosis. It retains the idea of *natura naturans*, or the Great Mother in its figuring of Nature. It rearranges the elements of creation myths, for example substituting the ocean for the garden but retaining the idea of the 'single progenitor' – though now an uncouth progenitor hard to acknowledge as kin. It foregrounds the concept of kin – and aroused many of the same dreads as fairy-tale in its insistence on the obligations of kinship, and the interdependence between beauty and beast. . . . In its insistence on chance as part of a deterministic order it perturbed in the same mode as *The Arabian Nights* – though more profoundly, because claiming the authority of science not exotic fiction. The pip thrown over the shoulder strikes the Grand Genie and vengeance ensues.

Gillian Beer, *Darwin's Plots* (1983), pp.9-10.

Beer rightly notes that the geologist Charles Lyell used the fifteenth book of Ovid's *Metamorphoses* and that the great French physiologist Claude Bernard cited Goethe (scientist and poet) repeatedly. Nor should we think of such allusions as casual, merely elegant decoration of scientific discourse; they can be highly significant.

At a crucial point in a lecture on 'Molecules' James Maxwell gave to the British Association (*Nature*, 25 September 1873), he saw fit to refer to Lucretius for his 'mental representation of the motion of atoms' as motes in a sunbeam shining through a darkened room. If we look up the passage, we discover that the Roman poet of science had foregrounded his own technique of giving a picture of the invisible and affording 'traces of a concept'. Elsewhere in *De Rerum Natura* he writes sophisticatedly of the general concepts we derive from experience which serve as 'anticipations' of future observations and discoveries (1947, Vol. 1, pp.53-54; 242-46). Maxwell, as we have seen, knew that this mental imaging, or combining of ideas with data, is a method of research. He continues in this lecture by quoting from Tennyson's adaptation of Lucretius, who in his dream of nature

> . . . saw the flaring atom-streams
> And torrents of her myriad universe,
> Ruining along the illimitable inane,
> Fly on to clash together again.
>
> 'Lucretius', *Macmillan's Magazine*, Vol. 18, 1868, p.2.

Maxwell employs this model of millions upon millions of irregular and unpredictable clashes to emphasise the impossibility of calculating the results of each and every collision. There can be no comparison with the dynamic calculation of forces in the visible everyday world. He then puts before his audience a practicable model of a different type, the Census: 'They begin by distributing the whole population into groups, according to age, income-tax, education, religious belief, or criminal convictions. . . . The varying number of individuals in each group, and not the varying state of each individual, is the primary datum from which they work.' He was therefore making use of literature and other patterns of meaning available in his culture to explain a new scientific approach to the understanding of molecular behaviour: 'The one may be called the historical, and the other the statistical method' (*Molecules*, p.440). Both create knowledge.

Maxwell's method allowed him to borrow, invent, test and modify a series of 'mental representations' of selected aspects of a complex universe, and discard them altogether if their 'anticipations' should prove to be inadequate. The habit of thought is fascinating and ingenious, to say the least, and definitely related to the literary imagination in its workings. Darwin too can write in a way that is as much literary as scientific:

> I cannot imagine any part of the world presenting a more extraordinary scene of the breaking up of the crust of the globe than the very central peaks of the Andes. The upheaval has taken place by a great number

of (nearly) N & S lines; which in most cases has formed
as many anticlinal & synclinal ravines: The strata in the
highest pinnacles are almost universally inclined at an
angle from 70°–80°. –
I cannot tell you how I enjoyed some of these views.
– it is worth coming from England once to feel such
intense delight. At an elevation from 10-12000 ft. there
is a transparency in the air & a confusion of distances &
a sort of stillness which gives the sensation of being in
another world, & when to this is joined, the picture so
plainly drawn of the great epochs of violence, it causes
in the mind a most strange assemblage of ideas.

Charles Darwin, *Correspondence* (1985), Vol. 1,
p.440.

Darwin's vision brings together an aesthetic response to the
visible landscape, full of 'Tumult and peace, . . . / The types
and symbols of Eternity' in the Romantic tradition
(Wordsworth, *The Prelude* (1805), Book 6, ll.567-71), and
that same landscape as a geological model of its own turbulent
history, which, he warns his correspondent at the beginning of
this long and conjectural letter of 18 April 1835, 'will appear to
you quite absurd & incredible'. But the precarious outward
movement of the mind in hypothesising is of its nature strange
and admirable, or the possible results would not be wonderful.
The fossilised trees he identifies in this letter are a minor
example; 'they consist of snow white columns Like Lots wife
of coarsely crystall. Carb. of Lime'.

As long as nineteenth-century scientists remained in a
shared discourse and culture, they used similar means to sway
their readers (see how the last paragraph of the *Origin* moves
from merely 'interesting' data to 'most beautiful and most
wonderful' evolution of forms), struggled with like problems
of literary expression and wrote with an imaginative sense of
fact, an ability to create potential truth, long thought typical of
men and women of letters. We need not collapse all
distinctions. Authors do not usually attempt to 'prove' literary
fictions, nor would we wish to discard them if it were possible
to 'falsify' them in some way. Nevertheless, the most

stimulating criticism at present assumes a genuine correspondence in ends and means so that, for instance, Redmond O'Hanlon reveals the deep concurrences between Conrad's *Lord Jim* (1900) and contemporary anthropology. That he drew upon Wallace's *The Malay Archipelago: The Land of the Orang-Utan and the Bird of Paradise* (1869) for certain scenes, incidents and the character of Stein is well known. He was probably acquainted with Max Nordau's extraordinary compilation of examples of European decline, translated under the title of *Degeneration* in 1895. But these are superficial connections in the light of O'Hanlon's analysis of Jim's retreat in evolutionary time to lands 'in the original dusk of their being' (Joseph Conrad, Lord Jim, Chapter 21), because he assumes a basic congruence between the scientific and the literary imaginations. If Conrad reminds us of Freud's models of mind, it is because they both thought about moral problems in the same basic way:

> The theory of the evolution of a moral sense leads at once to the theory of a conflict of instincts with different histories, fitted for different conditions; a conflict of times past with the present, the desires and needs of the pre-human creature and of savagery with those of civilised society; the desires of childhood with those of maturity. Conrad and Freud imagined (or discovered or created) an unconscious past – with their own distinctive personal and monstrous desires at play in it of course – but the murky landscape of that far country is much the same for both men.

> Redmond O'Hanlon, *Joseph Conrad and Charles Darwin* (1984), pp.47-48.

It is indeed knowledge that we are being given, by scientist and non-scientist alike. Wordsworth thought of it as discoveries about the world which would need humanising and transfiguring by the poet. Arnold, in similar vein, believed scientists came up with facts and general conceptions about the universe which then had to be related to our moral and aesthetic sense. Strangely, it is Blake with his assertion that scientists teach 'doubt & experiment' who comes closest to our modern position in these matters. Blake feared the constraints upon human imagination imposed by a narrowly rationalistic interpretation of life and the universe, but O'Hanlon's 'imagined (or discovered or created)' is as consistent with the practice of nineteenth-century scientists as it is with the old literary claim that the poet, in the general sense of one who possesses special creative power (*OED*, 1530), 'nothing affirmeth, and therefore never lieth'. Sir Philip Sidney was at one with men like Faraday, Maxwell, Darwin and Crookes and with all those writers who helped build the culture of their age. In this light Darwin's secluded Down House becomes a locus of creative thought as surely as Lady Gregory's house in the poetry of Yeats:

> I meditate upon a swallow's flight,
> Upon an aged woman and her house,
> A sycamore and lime-tree lost in night
> Although that western cloud is luminous,
> Great works constructed there in nature's spite
> For scholars and for poets after us,
> Thoughts long knitted into a single thought,
> A dance-like glory that those walls begot.

W.B. Yeats, 'Coole Park, 1929', stanza 1.

Chronological Table

This table has been compiled from a number of sources, but special mention should be made of the catalogue of Tennyson family libraries made by Nancie Campbell, *Tennyson in Lincoln*, Vol. 1 (Tennyson Society, Lincoln, 1971).

An asterisk before a title means that the work was first published in parts or as a serial.

Date	Contemporary events	Publications
1790		Buffon, *Les Époches de la Nature* (3rd edn)
1791		E. Darwin, *The Botanic Garden*
1792		Galvani, *De Viribus Electricitatis* J.E. Smith, *English Botany* (1790–1814) Walker, *Remarks Made in a Tour . . . to the Lakes*
1793	Pneumatic Institution, Bristol founded Newcastle Literary and Philosophical Society formed	
1794		Blake, *Songs of Innocence and Experience*
1795		E. Darwin, *Zoonomia* (1794–98) Blumenbach, *De Generis Humani Varietate Nativa* (3rd edn) Dupuis, *Origine de tous les Cultes* Euler, *Letters to a German Princess* (trans.) Hutton, *Theory of the Earth, With Proofs and Illustrations*
1796		Bonnycastle, *An Introduction to Astronomy* (3rd edn)

Date	Contemporary events	Publications
1796 cont.		Laplace, *Exposition du Système du Monde*
1797	Frere discovered flint implements at Hoxne in Suffolk	Bewick, *History of British Birds* (1797–1804)
1798	*Philosophical Magazine* (1798–1826)	Malthus, *An Essay upon the Principle of Population* Wordsworth and Coleridge, *Lyrical Ballads*
1799	Royal Institution founded Mineralogical Society formed Volta's battery (current electricity) invented	Walker, *A System of Familiar Philosophy*
1800	Act of Union with Ireland Volta wrote to Royal Society	Davy, *Researches, Chemical and Philosophical* M. Edgeworth, *Castle Rackrent*
1801	First English lecture theatre designed for science, in R.I. Société d'Arceuil (research centre) established	M. Edgeworth, *Frank* (introduction to science) Linneaus, *Elements of Natural History* (trans.)
1802	*Edinburgh Review* began First Factory Act Gay-Lussac's law of gases Peace of Amiens	Davy, *A Discourse, Introductory* Paley, *Natural Theology* Quincy, *Lexicon-medicum* (rev. edn) Scott, *Minstrelsy of the Scottish Border* (1802–1803)
1803	R.I. evening lectures began War with France	E. Darwin, *The Temple of Nature; or, The Origin of Society, a Poem, with Philosophical Notes* Imison, *Elements of science and art* (new edn)
1804	Napoleon crowned Emperor Horticultural Society formed	Blake, *Jerusalem* (1804–20) Parkinson, *Organic Remains of a Former World* (1804–11)
1805	Battles of Trafalgar, Ulm and Austerlitz Medical and Chirurgical Society founded	

Date	Contemporary events	Publications
1806		Bell, *Anatomy of Expression in Painting* Marcet, *Conversations on Chemistry* Parkes, *Chemical Catechism for the Use of Young People [with] Amusing Experiments*
1807	First public gas in London Geological Society formed	Crabbe, *Poems* (incl. 'Sir Eustace Grey') Hazlitt, *Reply to Malthus* T. Young, *A Course of Lectures on Natural Philosophy and the Mechanical Arts*
1808	*Examiner* began	Dalton, *A New System of Chemical Philosophy*
1809	*Quarterly Review* began Battle of Corunna	Joyce, *Scientific Dialogues* Lamarck, *Philosophie Zoologique*
1810		Crabbe, *The Borough* (incl. 'Peter Grimes')
1811	Prince of Wales made Regent Luddite Riots	Austen, *Sense and Sensibility* Cuvier and Brongniart, *Essai sur la Géographie Minéralogique des Environs de Paris*
1812	War with America (1812–14) Davy knighted for science (last occasion, Newton, 1705)	Cuvier, *Recherches sur les Ossemens Fossiles* Davy, *Elements of Chemical Philosophy*
1813	*Annals of Philosophy* began	Cuvier, *Essay on the Theory of the Earth* (trans.) Davy, *Agricultural Chemistry* Prichard, *Researches into the Physical History of Man* Shelley, *Queen Mab*
1814	End of American War Congress of Vienna Stephenson's locomotive	Humboldt, *Personal Narrative* (1814–29, trans.) Scott, *Waverley* Syme, *Werner's Nomenclature of Colours [for] Arts and Sciences* Wordsworth, *The Excursion*

Date	Contemporary events	Publications
1815	Battle of Waterloo Apothecaries' Act passed W. Smith's 'Geological Map of England' completed	Kett, *Elements of General Knowledge* (8th edn) Lamarck, *Histoire Naturelle* (1815–22) Malthus, *An Enquiry into Rent* Prout, *On the Relation between . . . Atoms*
1816	Spa Field Riot Davy's Safety Lamp designed	Byron, *The Siege of Corinth,* etc. Coleridge, *Christabel, Kubla Khan, The Pains of Sleep,* etc. Marcet, *Conversations on Political Economy* Peacock, *Headlong Hall*
1817	*Blackwood's Edinburgh Magazine* and *Literary Gazette* began	Coleridge, *Sibylline Leaves, Biographia Literaria* Ricardo, *Principles of Political Economy*
1818	Institution of Civil Engineers founded	Peacock, *Nightmare Abbey* Scott, *Rob Roy* M. Shelley, *Frankenstein*
1819	'Peterloo', Manchester	Byron, *Don Juan,* Cantos 1 and 2 Kant, *Prolegomena to Every Future Metaphysic* (trans.) Schopenhauer, *Die Welt als Wille und Vorstellung* [The World as Will and Idea]
1820	Accession of George IV *London Magazine* and *Retrospective Review* began Astronomical Society founded Oersted, Copenhagen, electrical deflection of compass needle	Thomas Brown, *Lectures on the Philosophy of the Human Mind* Godwin, *Of Population, An Answer to Malthus* Keats, *Lamia, Isabella, Eve of St Agnes,* etc. Malthus, *Principles of Political Economy* Peacock, *The Four Ages of Poetry* Shelley, *Prometheus Unbound*

Date	Contemporary events	Publications
1821	Death of Napoleon Faraday's electric motor Manchester Society for Natural History	Byron, *Cain* De Quincey, **Confessions of an English Opium Eater* Lucretius, *De Rerum Natura*, ed. G. Wakefield Mantell, *The Fossils of the South Downs* Shelley, *Adonais*
1822	Suicide of Castlereagh Deutscher Naturforscher Versammlung [German Natural Scientists' Assembly]	Byron, *The Vision of Judgement*, *Don Juan*, Cantos 1–5 Digby, *The Broad Stone of Honour* (1822–83) Shelley, *Hellas* Swainson, *The Naturalist's Guide for Collecting and Preserving*
1823	Meteorological Society Royal Manchester Institution Asiatic Society *The Lancet*, *The Phrenological Journal* and *The Quarterly Magazine* began Royal Society of Literature	Buckland, *Reliquae Diluvianae* Byron, *Heaven and Earth*, *Don Juan*, Cantos 6–14 Grimm brothers' fairy tales trans. (1823–26)
1824	London Mechanics' Institution founded *Westminster Review* began	Byron, *Don Juan*, Cantos 15–16 Carnot, *Réflexions sur la Puissance Motrice du Feu*
1825	Faraday's discovery of benzene	Coleridge, *Aids to Reflection* M. Edgeworth, *Harry and Lucy Concluded* Gall, *Sur les Fonctions du Cerveau* Hazlitt, *The Spirit of the Age* Laplace, *Mécanique Céleste* Thompson, *The Appeal of Women*
1826	University College London ('Literary and Scientific Education at a moderate expense') Society for the Diffusion of Useful Knowledge formed Zoological Society founded	Barrett, *An Essay on Mind, with Other Poems* Cooper, *The Last of the Mohicans*

Date	Contemporary events	Publications
1827	Death of Canning *Philosophical Magazine, or Annals of Chemistry* (1827–32)	Audubon, *The Birds of America* (1827–38) Cuvier, *The Animal Kingdom Arranged* (1827–35, trans.) W. Hamilton, *Notes to Assist the Memory in Various Sciences* (2nd edn) Hare brothers, *Guesses at Truth* (1827–48) Tennysons, *Poems by Two Brothers*
1828	Repeal of Test and Corporation Acts *Atheneum* and *Spectator* began Wöhler prepares urea artificially	Coleridge, *Poetical Works* Combe, *Constitution of Man* Niebuhr, *History of Rome* (1828–32, trans.) Von Baer, *Entwicklungsgeschichte der Thiere* [Developmental history of animals]
1829	Stephenson's *Rocket* Catholic Emancipation *La Revue des Deux Mondes* began	Barnes, *Etymological Glossary* Carlyle, 'Signs of the Times' Davy, *Consolations in Travel* J. Mill, *Analysis of the Human Mind* Tennyson, 'Timbuctoo' White, *Natural History of Selbourne* (new edn)
1830	Accession of William IV Geographical Society formed *Fraser's Magazine* began Manchester–Liverpool railway opened Duke of Sussex defeated J. Herschel for Royal Society's presidency	Babbage, *Reflections on the Decline of Science* Coleridge, *On the Constitution of the Church and State* Comte, *Cours de Philosophie Positive* (1830–42) Lyell, *Principles of Geology* (1830–33) Tennyson, *Poems, Chiefly Lyrical*
1831	Anatomy Act passed British Association for the Advancement of Science, York meeting	Brewster, *Treatise on Optics* J. Herschel, *Introduction to the Study of Natural Philosophy*

Date	Contemporary events	Publications
1831 cont.	Faraday's electromagnetic induction; began publishing *Experimental Researches* First Parliamentary Reform Bill	Peacock, *Crotchet Castle* St Hilaire, *Recherches sur de Grands Sauriens* Somerville, *Mechanism of the Heavens*
1832	BAAS, Oxford meeting Cholera epidemic England and Scotland Reform Act passed *The British Magazine, The Penny Magazine* and *The London and Edinburgh Philosophical Magazine* began	Christison, *A Treatise on Poisons* (2nd edn) Jameson, *Characteristics of Women* H. Martineau, *Illustrations of Political Economy* (1832–34) Tennyson, *Poems* ('1833')
1833	BAAS, Cambridge meeting Entomological Society formed Factory Act passed	Bridgewater Treatises (1833–37) Newman et al., *Tracts for the Times* (1833–37) Whewell, *Astronomy and General Physics*
1834	Abolition of Slavery in the British Empire Poor Law Amendment Act passed *The Penny Cyclopaedia*	Brewster, *Letters on Natural Magic . . . to Sir Walter Scott* Hawkins, *Memoirs of Ichthyosauri and Plesiosauri* Lindley, *Ladies' Botany* Lord, *Popular Physiology* Roget, *Animal and Vegetable Physiology* Somerville, *On the Connexion of the Physical Sciences*
1835	Telegraph invented	Browning, *Paracelsus* Dickens, *Sketches by Boz* 1 Elliotson, *Human Physiology* (5th edn)
1836	Botanical Society formed Flint tools found at Abbeville Stone, Bronze and Iron Ages proposed by Thomsen	Constable, *Fourth Lecture at the Royal Institution* Dickens, *Sketches by Boz* 2, *Pickwick Papers* (1836–37)
1837	Accession of Queen Victoria Daguerre's first photograph	Babbage, *Ninth Bridgewater Treatise* (uninvited) Thackeray, *Yellowplush Papers* Whewell, *History of the Inductive Sciences*

Date	Contemporary events	Publications
1838	Anti-Corn Law League, Manchester The People's Charter	Dickens, *Nicholas Nickleby* (1838–39) Mantell, *The Wonders of Geology*
1839	Anglo-Chinese Opium War began Microscopical Society formed Young England Movement	Carlyle, *Chartism* Faraday, *Experimental Researches in Electricity* (1839–55)
1840	Victoria marries Albert Penny Post Kew Gardens	Bulwer, *Money* Hawkins, *The Book of the Great Sea Dragons* Taylor, *The Natural History of Society* Whewell, *The Philosophy of the Inductive Sciences*
1841	Pharmaceutical Society formed Chemical Society formed Livingstone in Africa *Punch* began	Carlyle, *Heroes and Hero Worship* Dickens, *The Old Curiosity Shop*
1842	Mines Act passed Chadwick's Report on Sanitation Chartist Riots	Browning, *Dramatic Lyrics* W.B. Carpenter, *Principles of Human Physiology* Darwin, *Coral Reefs* Grove, 'Correlation of Physical Forces' Macaulay, *Lays of Ancient Rome* Tennyson, *Poems* (incl. 'Locksley Hall')
1843	Brunel's Thames tunnel opened Ethnological Society formed *The Zoist: A Journal of Cerebral Physiology and Mesmerism* began	Dickens, *A Christmas Carol* E. Jones, *Studies of Sensation and Event* Leslie, *Memoirs of the Life of John Constable* (1843–45) Ruskin, *Modern Painters* (1843–60)
1844	Factory Act passed Royal Commission on Health of Towns	Barnes, *Poems of Rural Life in the Dorset Dialect, Exercises in Practical Science* Chambers, *Vestiges of Creation* Kinglake, *Eothen*

Date	Contemporary events	Publications
1845	Irish Potato Famine British Museum Royal College of Chemistry	Browning, *Dramatic Romances and Lyrics* De Quincey, *Suspiria de Profundis* Disraeli, *Sybil* Humboldt, *Cosmos: a Sketch of a Physical Description of the Universe* (1851–52, trans.) Whewell, *Indications of the Creator*
1846	BAAS Ethnological Subsection Adams and Leverrier discovered Neptune's orbit First operation with general anaesthetic Railway boom began	Eliot, tr. Strauss, *Life of Jesus* Lear, *A Book of Nonsense* (1846–61) Melville, *Typee* Whewell, *Indications of the Creator* (2nd edn) Wittich, *Curiosities of Physical Geography*, Ser. 2, Earthquakes and Volcanoes
1847	Ten Hours Factory Act passed Institution of Mechanical Engineers Queenwood College	A. Brontë, *Agnes Grey* C. Brontë, *Jane Eyre* E. Brontë, *Wuthering Heights* Disraeli, *Tancred* Helmholtz, *Über die Erhaltung der Kraft* [On the Conservation of Force] Joule, 'On the Mechanical Equivalent of Heat' Lewes, *Ranthorpe* Mayer, *Beiträge zur Dynamik des Himmels* [Contributions to Celestial Dynamics] Tennyson, *The Princess* Thackeray, *Vanity Fair (1847–48)
1848	'Year of Revolutions' in Europe Public Health Act passed Queen's College for Women	Gaskell, *Mary Barton* J.S. Mill, *Principles of Political Economy* Thackeray, *The History of Pendennis (1848–50)

Date	Contemporary events	Publications
1849	Prince Albert visits R.I.	C. Brontë, *Shirley* Dickens, *David Copperfield* (1849–50) Ruskin, *Seven Lamps* Worsaae, *The Primeval Antiquities of Denmark* (trans.)
1850	Public Libraries Act passed Oxford Honours School in Natural Sciences *The Leader* began *Household Words* (1850–59)	Carlyle, *Latter-Day Pamphlets* Hawthorne, *The Scarlet Letter* Kingsley, *Alton Locke* Quekett, *Lectures on Histology* Stowe, *Uncle Tom's Cabin* Tennyson, *In Memoriam* Wordsworth, *The Prelude*
1851	Great Exhibition Owen's College, Manchester Australian Gold Rush	Carlyle, *The Life of John Sterling* Grimes, *Phreno-Geology* Mayhew, *London Labour and the London Poor* (1851–62) Melville, *Moby Dick* Ruskin, *Stones of Venice* (1851–53) Spencer, *Social Statics* D. Wilson, *The Archeology and Prehistoric Annals of Scotland*
1852	French Second Empire (1852–70)	Dickens, *Bleak House* (1852–53) Kelvin, 'Dissipation of Mechanical Energy' Spencer, 'The Developmental Hypothesis (20 March)
1853	Crimean War (1853–56) Department of Science and Art	W. Arnold, *Oakfield* W.B. Carpenter, *Principles of Human Physiology* (4th edn) Comte, *Positive Philosophy*, De Gobineau, *Essai sur l'Inégalité* (1853–55) Lewes, *Comte's Philosophy of the Sciences* Whewell, *Of the Plurality of Worlds*

Date	Contemporary events	Publications
1854	Working Men's College, London	Dickens, *Hard Times* Gaskell, *North and South* (1854–55) Thoreau, *Walden; or, Life in the Woods*
1855	Florence Nightingale in the Crimea	Browning, *Men and Women* Gatty, *Parables from Nature* (1855–65) Kingsley, *Glaucus; or, The Wonders of the Shore* (2nd edn) Knight, *The Plurality of Worlds* Spencer, *Principles of Psychology*
1856	Bessemer's steel process End of Crimean War National Police Force formed Perkin discovered aniline purple	
1857	Indian Mutiny Discovery of Neanderthal Man in Neandertal near Düsseldorf	E. Browning, *Aurora Leigh* (1857–59) Eliot, *Scenes of Clerical Life* Gaskell, *Life of Charlotte Brontë* P. Gosse, *Omphalos* Humphreys, *Ocean Gardens: the History of the Marine Aquarium* (2nd edn) Spencer, 'Progress: its Laws and Cause'
1858	Removal of Jewish disabilities	Barnes, *Hwomely Rhymes, Notes on Ancient Britain and the Britons* Ludlow, *British India: Its Races and Its History*
1859	Franco-Prussian War Kirchhoff and Bunsen discovered spectroscopy *Macmillan's Magazine* and *All the Year Round* began	Bain, *The Emotions and the Will* Bulwer, 'The Haunted and the Haunters' Collins, *The Woman in White* (1859–60) Darwin, *On the Origin of Species* Lewes, *The Physiology of Common Life* (1859–60)

Date	Contemporary events	Publications
1859 cont.		J.S. Mill, *On Liberty* Smiles, *Self-Help* Tennyson, *Idylls of the King* (1859–72)
1860	Food and Drugs Act passed Italian 'Risorgimento'	Eliot, *Mill on the Floss*, *Essays and Reviews* P. Gosse, *The Romance of Natural History* (1860–61) Lewes, *Studies in Animal Life* Peacock, *Gryll Grange*
1861	American Civil War began Death of the Prince Consort Pasteur's germ theory of disease	Maxwell, *On Physical Lines of Force* (1861–62) Müller, *Lectures on the Science of Language* (1861–64)
1862	Married Women's Property Act passed	Barnes, *Tiw; or, A View of the Roots and Stems of English* Kelvin, 'On the Age of the Sun's Heat' Kingsley, *The Water Babies* (1862–63) Spencer, *First Principles*
1863	Anthropological Society formed Institution of Gas Engineers formed	Gaskell, *Cousin Phyllis* Huxley, *Man's Place in Nature* Lyell, *The Antiquity of Man* Mayer, 'On Celestial Dynamics' (trans.) Sechenov, *The Reflexes of the Brain* (Russian)
1864	'Pasteurisation' X-Club (Huxley, Lubbock, Spencer, Tyndall et al.) formed	Browning, 'Caliban on Setebos' Collins, *Armadale* (1864–66) Gaskell, *Wives and Daughters* (1864–66) Spencer, *The Principles of Biology*
1865	End of American Civil War *Fortnightly Review* began Lister's antiseptic surgery Neolithic and Palaeolithic terms suggested	Bernard, *Introduction à l'Étude de la Médicine Expérimentale* Carroll, *Alice in Wonderland* Lubbock, *Prehistoric Times ... Modern Savages* Maxwell, *Dynamical Theory of the Electromagnetic Field*

Date	*Contemporary events*	*Publications*
1866	Mendel's laws of heredity, Brno publication Nobel's dynamite discovered	M. Arnold, *'The Study of Celtic Literature' Eliot, *Felix Holt* Hopkins, Journal kept 1866–75 Ruskin, *The Ethics of the Dust*
1867	Disraeli prime minister Paris Exhibition Pharmacy Act passed Second Reform Act passed	Bleek, *Über den Ursprung der Sprache* [On the Origin of Language] Clausius, *The Mechanical Theory of Heat* (trans.) Marx, *Das Kapital*
1868	Cro-Magnon Man discovered Gladstone prime minister Institution of Chartered Surveyors founded	Browning, *The Ring and the Book* (1868–69) Collins, *The Moonstone*
1869	*Nature* began Mendeleev's periodic table of the elements Suez canal The Metaphysical Society formed Iron and Steel Institute formed	Arnold, *Culture and Anarchy* Galton, *Hereditary Genius* Mill, *On the Subjection of Women* Ruskin, *The Queen of the Air* Wallace, *The Malay Archipelago*
1870	Franco-Prussian War (1870–71) Elementary Education Act passed Royal Commission on Scientific Instruction and the Advancement of Science (the Devonshire Commission)	Cobbe, 'Unconscious Cerebration' and 'Dreams' Dickens, *Edwin Drood* Disraeli, *Lothair* Gilbert, *The Princess . . . a Respectful Perversion, The Palace of Truth* Huxley, *Lay Sermons* Lubbock, *The Origin of Civilization and the Primitive Condition of Man* Tyndall, *Essays on the Use and Limit of the Imagination in Science*
1871	Anthropological Institute founded Newnham College, Cambridge opened	Bulwer, *The Coming Race* Caroll, *Alice Through the Looking-Glass* ('1872') Darwin, *The Descent of Man* Eliot, *Middlemarch* (1871–72)

Date	Contemporary events	Publications
1871 cont.	Institution of Electrical Engineers founded Institution of Telegraph Engineers founded	Gilbert, *Pygmalion and Galatea* (produced) Swinburne, *Songs Before Sunrise* Tylor, *Primitive Culture*
1872	Secret Ballot Act passed Edison's telegraph	Butler, *Erewhon* Darwin, *The Expression of the Emotions in Man and Animals* Hardy, **A Pair of Blue Eyes* Lang, *Ballads and Lyrics of Old France* W. Reade, *The Martyrdom of Man* Spencer, *The Principles of Psychology* (2nd edn)
1873	Cavendish Laboratory, Cambridge Sanky and Moody Revival Meetings	Helmholtz, *Popular Lectures on Scientific Subjects* (trans.) Maxwell, 'Molecules' Maudsley, *Body and Mind* (enlarged edn) Pater, *The Renaissance* (1873–77) Romanes, *Mental Evolution in Man* Somerville, *Personal Recollections* Spencer, *Descriptive Sociology* Stephen, *Essays in Freethinking and Plainspeaking*
1874	BAAS, Belfast meeting Disraeli prime minister Physical Society, London founded	W.B. Carpenter, *Principles of Mental Physiology* Galton, *English Men of Science: Their Nature and Nurture* Lewes, *Problems of Life and Mind* (1874–79) Lockyer, *Contributions to Solar Physics* Trollope, **The Way We Live Now* (1874–75) Tyndall, *Address* (to BAAS, Belfast meeting)

Date	Contemporary events	Publications
1875	Britain buys Suez Canal shares Theosophical Society founded	Clifford, *Body and Mind* Eddy, *Science and Health* Gilbert, *Trial by Jury* Wallace, *On Miracles and Modern Spiritualism*
1876	*Mind* began Victoria proclaimed Empress of India Edison's phonograph Telephone invented	Eliot, **Daniel Deronda* Haeckel, *The History of Creation* (trans.) James, **The American* (1876–77), **The Europeans* Hopkins, 'The Wreck of the Deutschland'
1877	Institute of Chemistry founded Annexation of the Transvaal *The Nineteenth Century* began	Dowden, 'The Scientific Movement in Literature' J. Hamilton, *Animal Futurity* Lewes, *The Physical Basis of Mind* Mallock, **The New Republic* Meredith, 'The Idea of Comedy, and of the Uses of the Comic Spirit' Morgan, *Ancient Society*
1878	Congress of Berlin Eddystone lighthouse London's electric street lighting Salvation Army founded	Hardy, *The Return of the Native* Gilbert, *H.M.S. Pinafore* Mallock, *The New Paul and Virginia, or Positivism on an Island*
1879	London's telephone exchange Gladstone's Midlothian campaign Wundt's Psychologisches Institut founded	Barnes, *Collected Poems* Browning, *Dramatic Idylls* 1 Butler, *Evolution Old and New* Haeckel, *The Evolution of Man* (trans.) Maudsley, *The Pathology of Mind* Spencer, *The Data of Ethics*
1880	Gladstone prime minister Transvaal declared itself a republic Metaphysical Society disbanded Physiological Society founded	Browning, *Dramatic Idylls* 2 Butler, *Unconscious Memory* James, **The Portrait of a Lady* (1880–81) Lankester, *Degeneration: A Chapter in Darwinism* Zola, *Le Roman Expérimental*

Date	Contemporary events	Publications
1881	Irish Land Act passed	Proctor, *The Poetry of Astronomy* 'Mark Rutherford', *Autobiography* Stevenson, *Treasure Island* (1881–82)
1882	Phoenix Park murders Daimler's petrol engine Society for Psychical Research founded Married Women's Property Act passed	Lang, *Helen of Troy* Trollope, *The Fixed Period*
1883	Royal College of Music founded	Blunt, *The Wind and the Whirlwind* Galton, *Inquiries into Human Faculty and Its Development* Jefferies, *The Story of My Heart* Maudsley, *Body and Will* Nietzsche, *Thus Spake Zarathustra*
1884	Third Reform Act passed *Oxford English Dictionary* (1884–1928) Fabian Society began BAAS, Montreal meeting	Gilbert, *Princess Ida* Huysman, *À Rebours* Lang, *Custom and Myth* (1884–85) Meredith, *Diana of the Crossways* (1884–85) Ruskin, 'The Storm Cloud of the Nineteenth Century'
1885	Fall of Khartoum	Clodd, *Myths and Dreams* Haggard, *King Solomon's Mines* Hutton, 'The Metaphysical Society: a Reminiscence' James, *The Bostonians* (1885–86) Jefferies, *After London* Kendall and Lang, 'That Very Mab' Ruskin, *Praeterita* (1885–89)
1886	Severn Tunnel opened	Nietzsche, *Beyond Good and Evil* Tennyson, *Locksley Hall Sixty Years After* Stevenson, *Dr. Jekyll and Mr. Hyde*

Date	Contemporary events	Publications
1887	Queen's Jubilee Edison's kinetoscope Michelson and Morley failed to detect ether by experiment *American Journal of Psychology* began Hertz discovered radio waves	W.B. Carpenter, *Mesmerism, Spiritualism, etc.* Haggard, *She* Lang, *Myth, Ritual and Religion* Meredith, *Ballads and Poems of Tragic Life* Müller, *The Science of Thought* Pater, *Imaginary Portraits* Stevenson, 'Memoir of Fleeming Jenkin'
1888	Kodak box camera Dunlop's pneumatic tyre	Clodd, *The Story of Creation* Kipling, *Plain Tales from the Hills, Soldiers Three* Moore, *Confessions of a Young Man* Yeats, *Fairy and Folk Tales of the Irish Peasantry* Zola, *La Terre*
1889	Institute of Marine Engineers founded Institution of Mining Engineers founded London Dock Strike First international congress of psychology, Paris *The New Review* began	E. Carpenter, *Civilization, its Cause and Cure* Galton, *Natural Inheritance* Gissing, *The Nether World* Wallace, *Darwinism* Weismann, *Essays upon Heredity* (trans.) Wilde, 'The Decay of Lying'
1890	British Astronomical Association founded First 'tube' railway Parnell scandal	Ellis, *The Criminal* Frazer, *The Golden Bough* (1890–1915) W. James, *Principles of Psychology* Morris, *News From Nowhere*
1891	Elementary education free	Hardy, *Tess of the d'Urbervilles* Lombroso, *The Man of Genius* (trans.) Wilde, *Intentions*; *The Picture of Dorian Gray*
1892	Institution of Mining and Metallurgy founded American Psychological Association formed	Hardy, *The Well-Beloved Henley, *The Song of the Sword* Kipling, *Barrack Room Ballads* Meredith, *Poems* Pearson, *The Grammar of Science*

Date	Contemporary events	Publications
1893	Manchester Ship Canal opened Benz's four-wheeled car	Kipling, *Many Inventions* Yeats, *The Celtic Twilight*
1894	Argon discovered Diesel engine invented Edison's Kinetoscope Parlour, New York	Drummond, *The Ascent of Man* Hardy, **Jude the Obscure* (1894–95) Kipling, *The Jungle Book* Moore, *Esther Waters* Morgan, *Introduction to Comparative Psychology*
1895	Helium discovered Röntgen's X-rays Marconi's wireless telegraphy Jameson Raid	Conrad, *Almayer's Folly* Freud, *Studies in Hysteria* L. Johnson, *Poems* Kipling, *The Second Jungle Book* Nordau, *Degeneration* (trans.) Wells, **The Time Machine, The Stolen Bacillus and Other Stories*
1896	Becquerel discovered radioactivity Langley's flying machine	Conrad, *An Outcast of the Islands* Kipling, *The Seven Seas* Stevenson, *Weir of Hermiston* Wells, *The Island of Dr. Moreau*
1897	J.J. Thomson discovered the electron Ross discovered the malaria bacillus Victoria's Diamond Jubilee	Conrad, *The Nigger of the 'Narcissus'* Lang, *Modern Mythology*; *The Book of Dreams and Ghosts* Pearson, *The Chances of Death* Ribot, *The Psychology of the Emotions* Stoker, *Dracula* Wells, *The Invisible Man*
1898	The Curies discovered radium Fashoda incident	Hardy, *Wessex Poems* James, **'The Turn of the Screw'* Lang, *The Making of Religion* Wells, *The War of the Worlds*

Chronological Table 181

Date	Contemporary events	Publications
1899	South African War (1899–1902) Rutherford named alpha and beta rays (uranium radiation) Irish Literary Theatre	Blunt, *Satan Absolved* Conrad, *'The Heart of Darkness' Symons, *The Symbolist Movement in Literature*
1900	Relief of Ladysmith and Mafeking Mendel's laws 'discovered' Planck's Quantum Theory	Conrad, *Lord Jim* Freud, *Interpretation of Dreams* Wallace, *Studies Scientific and Social* Wells, *Tales of Time and Space*
1901	Accession of Edward VII Marconi sent radio message across the Atlantic British Psychological Society founded Nobel prizes first awarded	Butler, *Erewhon Revisited* Shaw, *Man and Superman* Wells, *The First Men in the Moon*
1902	Education Act passed	Barrie, *The Admirable Crichton* (produced) W. James, *Varieties of Religious Experience* Kipling, *Just So Stories for Little Children*
1903		Butler, *The Way of All Flesh* James, *The Ambassadors*

A Guide to Reading

Primary Sources

A selection of titles available in modern editions is listed below:

Arnold, Matthew, *Complete Prose Works*, ed. R.H. Super, 11 vols (Ann Arbor, Michigan, University of Michigan Press, 1960–77) Vol. 3: 'On the Study of Celtic Literature; Vol. 7: *A Bible-Reading for Schools*; Vol. 10: 'Literature and Science'

Arnold, William, *Oakfield; or, Fellowship in the East* (2nd edn, 1854), ed. Kenneth Allott (Leicester University Press, 1973)

Blake, William, *Poems*, ed. W.H. Stevenson and D.V. Erdman (Longmans, 1971)

Browning, Robert, *Poetical Works*, eds Ian Jack and M. Smith, 2 vols (Oxford, Clarendon Press, 1983–84)

Byron, George Gordon, Lord, *Poetical Works*, ed. J.D. Jump (Oxford University Press, 1970)

Chambers, Robert, *Vestiges of the Natural History of Creation* (1844), ed. Gavin de Beer (Leicester University Press, 1969)

Coleridge, Samuel Taylor, *Biographia Literaria* (1817), ed. George Watson, 2 vols (Dent, 1978)

——, *Collected Letters*, ed. E.L. Griggs, 6 vols (Oxford, Clarendon Press, 1956–68)

——, *Poems*, ed. J.B. Beer (Dent, 1974)

Collins, Wilkie, *The Moonstone* (1868), ed. J.I.M. Stewart (Penguin, 1968)

Conrad, Joseph, *Heart of Darkness* (as 'The Heart of Darkness', 1899), intro. C.B. Cox (Dent, 1974)

Darwin, Charles, *Charles Darwin, Thomas Henry Huxley: Autobiographies*, ed. Gavin de Beer (Oxford University Press, 1974)

——, *The Correspondence of Charles Darwin*, ed. F. Burkhardt, Sydney Smith et al. (Cambridge University Press, 1985–   )

——, *On the Origin of Species by Means of Natural Selection* (1859), ed. J.W. Burrow (Penguin, 1968)

——, *The Descent of Man and Selection in Relation to Sex*, 2 vols 1871 (reprinted Brussels, Culture and Civilisation, 1969)

De Quincey, Thomas, *Confessions of an English Opium Eater* (1821), ed. Alethea Hayter (Penguin, 1971)

Dickens, Charles, *Bleak House* (1852–53), ed. Norman Page (Penguin, 1971)

——, *Edwin Drood* (1870), ed. M. Cardwell (Oxford University Press, 1972)

Disraeli, Benjamin, *Lothair* (1870), ed. V. Bogdanor (Oxford University Press, 1975)

Eliot, George, *Daniel Deronda* (1876), ed. G. Handley (Oxford University Press, 1984)

——, *Middlemarch* (1871–72), ed. W.J. Harvey (Penguin, 1965)

Gosse, Edmund, *Father and Son: A Study of Two Temperaments* (1907), ed. James Hepburn (Oxford University Press, 1974)

Hardy, Thomas, *The Complete Poems*, ed. James Gibson (Macmillan, 1976)

——, *The Mayor of Casterbridge* (1886), (Macmillan, 1958)

——, *A Pair of Blue Eyes* (1872–73) ed. Alan Hanford (Oxford University Press, 1985)

——, *Tess of the d'Urbervilles* (1891) (Macmillan, 1968)

Heath-Stubbs, John and Salman, Phillips (eds), *Poems of Science* (Penguin, 1984). Includes poems by E. Darwin, Pindar, Blake, Wordsworth, Coleridge, Hoare, Davy, Byron, Shelley, Keats, Beddoes, Emerson, Turner, Holmes, Poe, Tennyson, Browning, Clough, Melville, Whitman, Arnold, Patmore, Meredith, Dickinson, Maxwell, Thomson, Swinburne, Hardy, Blind, Bridges, Hopkins and Kipling.

Herschel, Sir J.F.W. *A Preliminary Discourse on the Study of National Philosophy*, 1831, intro. Michael Partridge (New York, Johnson Reprint Corporation, 1966)

Hopkins, Gerard Manley, *Poems* (1918), eds W.H. Gardner and N.H. Mackenzie (Oxford University Press, 1967)

Kingsley, Charles, *Alton Locke* (1850), ed. E.A. Cripps (Oxford University Press, 1983)

——, *The Water Babies* (1862–63), (Dent, 1957)

Lewes, George Henry, *Ranthorpe* (1847), ed. Barbara Smalley (Athens, Ohio University Press, 1974)

Lyell, Charles, *Principles of Geology, being an Attempt to Explain the Former Changes of the Earth's Surface by Reference to Causes Now in Operation*, 3 vols 1830–33 intro. M.J.S. Rudwick (Codicot, Wheldon and Wesley, 1970)

Mallock, William Hurrell, *The New Republic: Culture, Faith and Philosophy in an English Country House* (1876), intro. John Lucas (Leicester University Press, 1975)

Meredith, George, *Poems*, ed. Phyllis B. Bartlett, 2 vols (New Haven, Yale University Press, 1978)

Peacock, Thomas Love, *Crotchet Castle* (1831), ed. R. Wright (Penguin, 1969)

——, *Melincourt* (1817), in *Novels*, ed. D. Garnett, Vol. 1 (2nd edn, Rupert Hart-Davis, 1963)

Shelley, Mary, *Frankenstein* (1818), ed. M.K. Joseph (Oxford University Press, 1971)

Shelley, Percy Bysshe, *Poetical Works*, ed. T. Hutchinson and G.M. Matthews (Oxford University Press, 1970)

Tennyson, Alfred, Lord, *Poems*, ed. Christopher Ricks (Longmans, 1969)

Thackeray, William Makepeace, *Vanity Fair* (1847–48), ed. John Sutherland (Oxford University Press, 1983)

Wells, Herbert George, *The First Men in the Moon* (1901), intro. F. Wells (1951)

——, *The Island of Doctor Moreau* (1896), in *Three Novels* (Heinemann, 1963)

——, *Selected Short Stories* (Penguin 1958). Includes 'The Time Machine', 'The Stolen Bacillus', 'The Remarkable Case of Davidson's Eyes' and 'The Lord of the Dynamos'

Whewell, William, *The Philosophy of the Inductive Sciences*, 3 vols (1840). Facsimile of 2nd edn (1847), 2 vols, intro. J. Herivel (New York and London, Johnson Reprint Corporation, 1967)

Wilde, Oscar, *Complete Works*, ed. and intro. V. Holland (Collins, 1966)

Wordsworth, William, *Poetical Works*, eds T. Hutchinson and E. de Selincourt (Oxford University Press, 1969)

Secondary Sources, Introductory

Cosslett, Tess, *The 'Scientific Movement' and Victorian Literature* (Harvester Press, 1982)

Gross, John, *The Rise and Fall of the Man of Letters: Aspects of English Literary Life since 1800* (Weidenfeld and Nicolson, 1969)

Huxley, Aldous, *Literature and Science* (Chatto and Windus, 1963)

Knight, David M., *The Nature of Science: the History of Science in Western Culture since 1600* (André Deutsch, 1976)

——, *Sources for the History of Science 1660–1914* (Cambridge University Press, 1975)

Oldroyd, David R., *Darwinian Impacts: An Introduction to the Darwinian Revolution* (Milton Keynes, Open University Press, 1980) (Exceptional coverage, valuable.)

Stonyk, Margaret, *Nineteenth-Century English Literature* (Macmillan, 1983) (With useful bibliography.)

Further Reading 1

Allott, Miriam, *Novelists on the Novel* (Routledge, 1959)

Altick, R.D., *Victorian People and Ideas* (New York, Norton, 1973; Dent, 1974)

Ball, Patricia M., *The Science of Aspects: the Changing Role of Fact in the Work of Coleridge, Ruskin and Hopkins* (Athlone Press, 1971)

Beer, Gillian, *Darwin's Plots: Evolutionary Narrative in Darwin, George Eliot and Nineteenth-Century Fiction* (Routledge and Kegan Paul, 1983)

Butler, Marilyn, *Romantics, Rebels and Reactionaries: English Literature and its Background, 1760–1830* (Oxford University Press, 1981)

Cannon, S.F., *Science in Culture: The Early Victorian Period* (New York, Dawson and Science History Publications, 1978)

Carlyle, Thomas, 'Signs of the Times', Anon, *Edinburgh Review*, Vol. 49, 1829, pp. 439-49 in *Selected Writings*, ed. Alan Shelston (Penguin, 1971)

Conrad, Joseph, Preface, *The Nigger of the 'Narcissus'* (*New Review*, 1897)

Cosslett, Tess (ed.), *Science and Religion in the Nineteenth Century* (Cambridge University Press, 1984) Substantial selections from Paley, Chambers, Miller, Darwin (*Origin* and *Descent*), Goodwin, L. Huxley, Tyndall and Temple.

Eiseley, Loren, *Darwin's Century: Evolution and the Men who Discovered It* (Doubleday, 1958)

Ellman, R. and Feidelson, C. (eds), *The Modern Tradition: Backgrounds to Modern Literature* (New York, Oxford University Press, 1965) (Substantial, European scope.)

Gillispie, Charles C., *The Edge of Objectivity: An Essay on the History of Scientific Ideas* (Princeton University Press, 1960)

Greene, John C., *The Death of Adam: Evolution and its Impact on Western Thought* (Ames, Iowa State University Press, 1959)

Houghton, Walter E., *The Victorian Frame of Mind 1830–1870* (New Haven, Yale University Press, 1957)

Levere, Trevor H., *Poetry Realised in Nature: Samuel Taylor Coleridge and Early Nineteenth-Century Science* (Cambridge University Press, 1981)

Millhauser, M., *Just Before Darwin: Robert Chambers and 'Vestiges'* (Middletown, Wesleyan University Press, 1959)

———, *Fire and Ice: The Influence of Science on Tennyson's Poetry* (Lincoln, The Tennyson Society, 1971)

Morton, Peter, *The Vital Science: Biology and the Literary Imagination 1860–1900* (Allen and Unwin, 1985)

Roppen, George, *Evolution and Poetic Belief: A Study in Some Victorian and Modern Writers* (Oslo, 1956)

Whyte, L.L., *The Unconscious Before Freud* (New York, Basic Books, 1960; Tavistock Publications, 1967)

Further Reading 2

Baker, John R., *Race* (Oxford University Press, 1974)

Bowler, Peter J., *Evolution: The History of An Idea* (Berkeley, University of California Press, 1984)

Brooks, John L., *Just Before the Origin: Alfred Russel Wallace's Theory of Evolution* (New York, Columbia University Press, 1984)

Burchfield, Joe D., *Lord Kelvin and the Age of the Earth* (Macmillan, 1975)

Burrow, John W., *Evolution and Society: A Study in Victorian Social Theory* (Cambridge University Press, 1966)

Chant, C. and Fauvel, J. (eds), *Darwin to Einstein: Historical Studies on Science and Belief* (Harlow, Longman, 1980)

Desmond, Adrian, *Archetypes and Ancestors: Palaeontology in Victorian London 1850–1875* (Blond and Briggs, 1982) (More scope than its sub-title suggests.)

Gillespie, Neal C., *Charles Darwin and the Problem of Creation* (University of Chicago Press, 1979)

Goldman, Martin, *The Demon in the Aether: The Story of James Clerk Maxwell* (Edinburgh, Paul Harris Publishing, 1983)

Gould, Stephen Jay, *Ontogeny and Phylogeny* (Cambridge, Mass., Harvard University Press, 1977)

Greene, M.T. Geology in the Nineteenth Century: Changing Views of a Changing World (Ithaca, Cornell University Press, 1982)

Gruber, H.E. and Barrett, P.H., *Darwin on Man: A Psychological Study of Scientific Creativity together with Darwin's Early and Unpublished Notebooks* (New York, Dutton, 1974)

Hayter, Alethea, *Opium and the Romantic Imagination* (Faber, 1968)

Henkin, Leo J., *Darwinism in the English Novel, 1860–1910: The Impact of Evolution on Victorian Fiction* (New York, Russell and Russell, 1940, 1963)

Hunter, Allan, *Joseph Conrad and the Ethics of Darwinism: The Challenges of Science* (Croom Helm, 1983)

Hyman, Stanley E., *The Tangled Bank: Darwin, Marx, Frazer and Freud as Imaginative Writers* (New York, Atheneum, 1962)

Killham, John, *Tennyson and 'The Princess': Reflections of an Age* (Athlone Press, 1958)

King-Hele, Desmond, *Erasmus Darwin and the Romantic Poets* (Macmillan, 1985)

Knight, David M., *The Transcendental Part of Chemistry* (Folkestone, Dawson, 1978)

Leaf, Murray G., *Man, Mind, and Science: A History of Anthropology* (New York, Columbia University Press, 1979)

Magner, Lois N., *A History of the Life Sciences* (New York and Basel, 1979)

Medawar, Peter, *Pluto's Republic* (Oxford University Press, 1982)

Morrell, J, and Thackray A. (eds), *Gentlemen of Science: The Origins and Early Years of the British Association for the Advancement of Science* (Oxford University Press, 1981)

O'Hanlon, Redmond, *Joseph Conrad and Charles Darwin: The Influence of Scientific Thought on Conrad's Fiction* (Edinburgh, Salamander Press, 1984)

Oldroyd, David and Langham, I. (eds), *The Wider Domain of Evolutionary Thought* (Dordrecht, D. Reidel Publishing Company, 1983)

Ospovat, Dov, *The Development of Darwin's Theory: Natural History, Natural Theology, and Natural Selection 1838–1859* (Cambridge University Press, 1981)

Paradis, J. and Postlewait, T. (eds), *Victorian Science and Victorian Values: Literary Perspectives* (New York, Academy of Sciences, 1981)

Patterson, Elizabeth C., *Mary Somerville and the Cultivation of Science, 1815–1840* (Boston, etc., Martinus Nijhoff Publishers, 1983)

Rupke, Nicolaas A., *The Great Chain of History: William Buckland and the English School of Geology 1814–1849* (Oxford University Press, 1983)

Rousseau, G.S., 'Literature and Science: the State of the Field', *Isis*, Vol. 69 (1978), pp. 583–91. (A survey of secondary works since 1950.)

Russel, Colin A., *Science and Social Change 1700–1900* (Macmillan, 1983)

Samburdsky, S., *Physical Thought from the Presocratics to the Quantum Physicists: An Anthology* (Hutchinson, 1974)

Sharlin, H.I., *Lord Kelvin: the Dynamic Victorian* (Pennsylvania State University Press, 1979)

Shuttleworth, Sally, *George Eliot and Nineteenth-Century Science: The Make-Believe of a Beginning* (Cambridge University Press, 1984)

Stocking, George W., *Race, Culture, and Evolution: Essays in the History of Anthropology* (New York, The Free Press, 1968)

Street, Brian V., *The Savage in Literature: Representations of 'Primitive' Society in English Fiction 1850–1920* (Routledge and Kegan Paul, 1975)

Teich, M. and Young, R.M. (eds), *Changing Perspectives in the History of Science: Essays in Honour of Joseph Needham* (Heinemann, 1973)

Young, R.M., *Darwin's Metaphor: Nature's Place in Victorian Culture* (Cambridge University Press, 1985)

Index